# PLATONIC IDEAS IN SPENSER

# Platonic Ideas in Spenser

BY

MOHINIMOHAN BHATTACHERJE, M.A., PH.D.

PREMCHAND ROYCHAND STUDENT,
Author of 'Studies in Spenser'

WITH A FOREWORD

BY

ÉMILE LEGOUIS

HONORARY PROFESSOR OF ENGLISH LITERATURE, THE SORBONNE, PARIS

GREENWOOD PRESS, PUBLISHERS
WESTPORT, CONNECTICUT

Originally published in 1935
by Longmans, Green & Co., Ltd., London

First Greenwood Reprinting 1970

Library of Congress Catalogue Card Number 73-98858

SBN 8371-3129-4

Printed in the United States of America

TO

THE REVERED MEMORY

OF

SIR ASUTOSH MOOKERJEE

# PREFACE

THIS dissertation attempts to trace Platonic and Neo-Platonic ideas in the poetry of Edmund Spenser and is based mainly on a detailed study of his works and the Dialogues of Plato together with some of the *Enneads* of Plotinus. It was submitted, along with another dissertation, as a thesis for the Doctorate of Philosophy in the University of Calcutta but has since gone through a few alterations.

Platonism was specially congenial to the spirit of Spenser and Platonic influence in his Hymns had been noticed quite early. But a detailed study of his Platonism began only recently in America, and it is worthy of note that American scholarship has made remarkable contributions to it. Scholars and critics in Europe too have pursued the study of the topic with evident interest. I have derived considerable help from the results of the labours of many and have duly acknowledged my obligation to them.

The problem of Platonic influence in the *Faerie Queene* has recently grown complicated on account of the importance given by some critics to the wording of Spenser's Letter to Raleigh. The Introduction and Chapter I of the present volume contain a discussion of the question, but its satisfactory solution is certainly difficult. In Chapters II and III, I have ventured to differ from some well-known scholars in my interpretation of Spenser's conceptions of Chastity and Holiness. In Chapter VI special attention has been drawn to Italian Neo-Platonists; but Giordano Bruno has been left out, as I dealt with the question of his influence on the English poet in my other dissertation entitled *Studies in Spenser* already published by the University of Calcutta. Platonism in the *Amoretti,* as distinct from Petrarchism which has frequently been the subject of critical study, has been traced to French sonneteers of the sixteenth century in Chapter VIII.

In conclusion, I have to express my deep obligation to M. Émile Legouis, the distinguished scholar and critic and Honorary Professor of English Literature in the University of Paris, for his great kindness in contributing the 'Foreword' to this volume. I also take this opportunity of conveying my thanks to some of my friends and my colleagues in the University of Calcutta who took the trouble of reading the proofs.

*Department of English,*
*University of Calcutta;* M. M. BHATTACHERJE.
*September,* 1934.

# FOREWORD

I WISH that a critic better qualified than myself should have written the 'Foreword' to this remarkable book. I have expressed at some length my admiration of Edmund Spenser as a poet or, more precisely, as one of the greatest word-painters, but have confessed that my interest in his philosophy did not rise very high. The philosopher in him is merely a disciple of the ancients, somewhat hesitating and perplexed between his pagan masters and the teaching of Christianity. The poet is unique and supreme in many respects.

But I never meant to imply that his debt to Aristotle and chiefly to Plato did not deserve careful investigation. His borrowings from Plato are obvious and have often been pointed out. They are mostly prominent in his Hymns, but not confined to them alone. They can scarcely be exaggerated. It curiously happens that as I was setting to write the few words of this 'Foreword', I received a new publication of the John Hopkins Press: *The Axiochus of Plato translated by Ed. Spenser in 1592.* The *Axiochus* is no longer attributed to Plato but it was so by all commentators in the sixteenth century and the translation affords a fresh proof of Spenser's

# FOREWORD

Platonism. Spenser believed that he was reproducing the very thoughts of his Greek master 'concerning the shortnesse and uncertainty of this life, with the ends of the good and the wicked'.

Of course, this quite recent discovery could not be known to Mr. Bhattacherje when he composed his thesis. But it comes somehow in confirmation of his subject and of his views. The coincidence seems to add a piquancy to his distinguished work.

Yet there is in his volume a novelty of much broader significance. It shows how thoroughly English literature is now being studied in India, and by Indians. Essays like the one under consideration are no longer summaries or replicas of European researches but personal and original examinations of special problems. Eastern scholars now bring in trained minds to inquiries and controversies which had till recently been monopolised by the West. I for one expect much from their collaboration. Thus will the intellectual and literary outlooks of Orient and Occident be gradually enlarged for the good of the two hemispheres.

ÉMILE LEGOUIS<br>
Professeur honoraire à<br>
la Sorbonne

# CONTENTS

| Chap. | | Page |
|---|---|---|
| | Preface ... ... ... | vii |
| | Foreword ... ... ... | ix |
| | Introduction ... ... ... | 1 |

## PLATONISM

| | | |
|---|---|---|
| I. | Blending of the Ideas of Plato and Aristotle—Temperance ... ... | 20 |
| II. | Chastity ... ... ... | 46 |
| III. | Truth ... ... ... | 71 |
| IV. | Friendship ... ... ... | 107 |

## NEO-PLATONISM

| | | |
|---|---|---|
| V. | Theories of Beauty and Love ... | 115 |
| VI. | Heavenly Love ... ... ... | 150 |
| VII. | Mysticism—Heavenly Beauty ... | 162 |
| VIII. | The *Amoretti* ... ... ... | 177 |
| | Bibliography ... ... ... | 196 |

# INTRODUCTION

SPENSER lived at the junction of two epochs in the history of Europe and was subject to many influences—literary, religious and moral—of both. As Legouis says, 'His poetry, like his own thought, was a battle-field. In his verse the classic Renaissance and religious Reform ride against each other with spears couched, like the knights in his many jousts and tournaments. . . . His cherished faith was Platonism, which makes beauty the divine soul of the world. And yet this imagination, this faith, were always repressed and held in check by the Christian sense of the vanity of all sensual delights.' 'The Middle Ages, with their allegories or moralities, with their romances of chivalry, mainly from the Arthurian cycle, there meet with classical mythology, which is seen in turn through the eyes of the Renaissance.'[1]

A study of any particular aspect of his life or of his works is, therefore, difficult, as it involves the separation of this aspect from others with which it is closely connected. It is, in a sense, also misleading, as it may convey the impression

[1] Legouis' *Spenser*, p. 120.

that nothing else in connection with his life or his works is important. It is not, therefore, altogether superfluous to point out that the present study in Platonic and Neo-Platonic influences on Spenser is not intended to belittle or to ignore other influences on him or the broader aspects of his mind and thought. It just leaves them out of consideration together with the artistic merits and literary antecedents of his poetry. But there is a further risk of misapprehension. The Middle Ages looked upon the different aspects of human life and human interests as separate, unconnected matters. But 'this separation of human functions and interests could not last for ever, and when it weakened, there began the Renaissance, the discovery of man as a whole, indivisible, mind and body and soul together—the discovery of the central inclusive fact of life.'[1] Spenser had drunk deep of the spirit of his age and was interested in life above everything else. An attempt to trace philosophic ideas in the works of such a poet may very well be regarded as involving an implication about the narrowness of his interests and his adherence to a school. But no such inference should be possible when Plato's influence is in question.

[1] Renwick's *Edmund Spenser*, p. 152.

# INTRODUCTION 3

It was because Spenser was a lover not of theory only but of life in all its mysteriousness and possibilities that he turned to Plato and Lucretius—one a philosopher who was also a poet and the other a poet who was also a philosopher.

Spenser has often been called the child of the Renaissance. But his greatest work bears a distinct impress of the Middle Ages, both in its manner and in its matter. Chivalry furnishes the background of the story of the *Faerie Queene* which unrolls the brilliant pageantry and phantasmagoria of the mediaeval world. The digressions, the long-drawn-out descriptions of courts and battle-fields and the exposition of moral and religious ideas remind one of the diffuse style of the mediaeval romances. Traces of the Renaissance in Spenser have therefore to be sought for elsewhere, and his Platonism may be described as summing up the main influence of the Renaissance on the English poet. The Renaissance had first affected England as a religious awakening which was a protest against the corruption and the rigours of the Church. A quickening of sympathy, an interest in the well-being of mankind, a keen sense of beauty—these effects of the movement manifested themselves later as the outcome of the revival of classical learning

## 4   PLATONIC IDEAS IN SPENSER

in a class of people different from the religious reformers. In Spenser, however, both these aspects of the new movement are equally noticeable.[1] The influence of Plato which Spenser imbibed as the result of his classical studies, not only dignified his conception of beauty and broadened his sympathy, but also added to his moral enthusiasm.

The channels through which Platonism and Neo-Platonism reached Spenser may be briefly indicated. Though based on a study of Plato in the original, which was a special feature of the Cambridge University[2] when Spenser joined it in 1569, Spenser's Platonism, different as it was from the Christianised Neo-Platonism of the so-called Dionysius,[3] was yet tinged with the Neo-Platonism of Plotinus. For 'Platonism had been strangely transformed by its passage through the Neo-Platonism of Alexandria' and the teachings of Plato as received in Europe during the Renaissance, were 'intermixed and confused with the mysticism of Philo and Plotinus, and with ideas

---

[1] Dowden's *Spenser, the Poet and Teacher*.
[2] See Courthope's *History of English Poetry*, Vol. II. p. 240.
[3] *Cambridge History of English Literature*, Vol. III. p. 214.

# INTRODUCTION

derived from the Jewish Cabala, and even from Indian and Egyptian sources'.[1] Marsilio Ficinus was a well-known interpreter of Plato in that age. He had translated Plato's dialogues and the *Enneads* of Plotinus into Latin and in his Latin commentary on the *Symposium* (*Commentarium in Convivium*) had discussed and illustrated 'Plato's meaning in the light of the Neo-Platonists, and of Plotinus in especial'.[2] An Italian version of this commentary was also well-known. Spenser derived many of his Platonic ideas from the commentary of Ficinus. Pico della Mirandola was, like Ficinus, another interpreter of Plato in the light of Neo-Platonism. His treatise entitled *A Platonick Discourse upon Love* written as a commentary on Benivieni's Sonnet entitled *Ode of Love* (which was based on the emanation-theory of Plotinus) and published along with it in 1487 and the dissertations in the Neo-Platonic vein on the Platonic ideas of love and beauty in the Italian courtesy-books of the 15th century, also received the attention of Spenser. The *Cortegiano* was the most important of these courtesy-

---

[1] L. Winstanley's *Introduction* to Spenser's *Fowre Hymnes*, p. x.
[2] *Ibid.* p. lviii.

## 6   PLATONIC IDEAS IN SPENSER

books and Bembo's oration on love in it was inspired by the disquisitions in *Degli Asolani* and was followed in later works of a similar nature, e.g., Annibale Romei's *Discorsi*. The Nolan philosopher Giordano Bruno who was inspired by Plato's mystic ideals of love and beauty and who visited England in 1583-5 and lectured at Oxford, possibly influenced the English poet. Finally, the form in which the French sonneteers of the Pléiade expressed the Neo-Platonic ideas of some of these Italian writers, left its trace in the *Amoretti*.

It would be unusual to-day to doubt Spenser's knowledge of Plato; yet a writer in the *Modern Language Review,* on noticing some wrong references to the *Critias* in the *Faerie Queene,*[1] has suggested[2] that Spenser was not acquainted even with the *Phaedo,* but had merely read some works of Cicero containing discussions on Plato. On the other hand, there are critics who, while admitting Spenser's close knowledge of Plato, argue that the poet was not influenced by the philosophy of Plato in any sense. Literary imita-

---

[1] Bk. II. C. VII. st. 54 and Bk. IV. Introductory Stanza 3.
[2] Vol. XIX. p. 208.

# INTRODUCTION 7

tion was very common during the 16th century and Spenser did imitate ideas—and phrases too—from a host of predecessors,—Lucretius, Aristotle, Ronsard, Marot, Tasso, Bembo. 'Use of quotations', it is argued, 'may be proof of study, but is not necessarily proof of intellectual discipleship, still less of complete acceptance of a system of thought'.[1] Spenser's object, we are told, was 'literary imitation and careful exhibition of wide scholarship', not theorising. 'The difficulty—and the interest—arises from his (Spenser's) equal acceptance of all available authorities. It should not be increased by over-simplification, by trying to confine Spenser to a school'.[2] Conviction depends on temperament and the same evidence cannot possibly satisfy all. But the possibility of Plato's influence cannot be ruled out merely by pointing out the existence of Aristotle's conceptions and Lucretius' imagery side by side with Platonic ideas in Spenser. A versatile mind like Spenser's could very well imbibe and appreciate different and even contradictory theories without subscribing to any one of them as fully convincing and infallible. As Renwick says, 'He

---

[1] Renwick's *Edmund Spenser*, p. 154.
[2] *Ibid.* p. 161.

could accept all the ancient *schools,* all that the ancients believed to be true, just because they were all equally superseded by revealed religion. The fundamental fact about his ethics is that they were those of a Christian, a Protestant Christian with a tendency . . . towards Calvinism."[1] An attempt has recently been made to stress Spenser's obligations to Lucretius and Ovid and to put them at least on a par with the poet's debt to Plato.[2] The present study is not concerned with these Latin poets, but it seems that the importance given to their influence is excessive.

Some are of opinion[3] that Spenser was influenced only by Plato's theories of love and beauty, and only the Hymns of Spenser are mentioned by them as illustrating his Platonism. But the *Faerie Queene,* the *Shepheards Calender* and some of his other poems, too, show the impress of Platonic ideas on Spenser's thought; and these include other notions besides the famous conceptions of love and beauty. Some critics have made too much of Spenser's well-known Letter to

---

[1] Renwick's *Edmund Spenser*, p. 161.
[2] *Ibid.* ch. VI.
[3] See Hales' Memoir of Spenser in the Globe Edition of his Works, p. liii.

# INTRODUCTION 9

Raleigh and argued, on the strength of his admission made in it, that the *Faerie Queene* with its allegories of Temperance, Chastity, etc. is a mere exposition of the *Nicomachean Ethics*. Considerable support seems to be given to this view by the conversation which Spenser had in Ireland with Lodovick Bryskett when he was engaged in composing the *Faerie Queene* which, according to Spenser himself, was meant 'to represent all the moral vertues' as discussed in the 'Ethicke part of Morall Philosophie' by which the poet obviously referred to Aristotle's *Ethics*. This conversation is reported in Bryskett's work entitled *A Discourse of Civill Life*.[1] But it would be a mistake to pin Spenser down to the wording of his letter and to interpret the admission contained in it as excluding the possibility of every influence other than Aristotle's. Traces of Plato's ideas are clear in the *Faerie Queene*, though his obligation to Plato was not expressly acknowledged by Spenser as Aristotle's influence was. One reason why Spenser described himself as a debtor of Aristotle seems to be this, viz., that authors in his days liked to be known as followers of renowned precedents and Spenser's literary

[1] See Hales' Memoir, p. xxxiii.

masters, Ariosto and Tasso, were both taken to have allegorised Aristotle's moral (as well as political) virtues.[1] The authors of Italian courtesy-books which had the same didactic aim as Spenser's poem, viz., 'to fashion a gentleman in vertuous and gentle discipline' and to some of which Spenser was indebted for his ideas of love, though following Ficinus' and Pico's interpretation of Plato's theory of love, bestowed the moral virtues of Aristotle on their ideal gentleman. The moral excellence insisted on in the *Cortegiano*, for instance, is derived from the *Ethics*.[2] *Il Nennio* expounds at length the doctrine of the mean. In Muzio's *Gentilhuomo* the emphasis laid on good birth and virtue as the mark of a typical courtier is also Aristotelian in origin, as is likewise the doctrine of the mean.[3] Guazzo in his *Civil Conversations* bitterly complains against the indifference with which the Aristotelian virtue of good birth was apt to be regarded by people in his days.[4] A second reason for Spenser's declaration

---

[1] See Spenser's Letter to Raleigh.
[2] *Modern Language Review*, Vol. V. p. 150.
[3] *Ibid.* Vol. V. p. 159.
'Some things there are, again, a deficiency in which mars blessedness—good birth, for instance, or fine offspring, or even personal beauty '.—*Ethics*, Bk. I. ch. IX.
[4] Einstein's *Italian Renaissance in England*, p. 63.

## INTRODUCTION

of his obligation to Aristotle seems to have been the regard in which this moral philosopher was held by Christian theologians, both Catholic and Protestant. St. Thomas and Melanchthon both tried to base Christian ethics on the speculations of the Greek philosopher. A tradition of Christian Aristotelianism had grown up in Europe during the Middle Ages,[1] and Spenser undoubtedly desired to offer his homage to the ancient teacher of moral virtue which, as an ardent Calvinist, he valued so much. Another reason for an express declaration of the poet's obligation to Aristotle to the exclusion of Plato, is probably to be found in the fact that Aristotle impressed the young Spenser more strongly than Plato, though his acquaintance with both these philosophers might have begun simultaneously, viz., about the year 1569 when he joined Cambridge.[2] The intellectual faculty is sometimes stronger in youth than the power of contemplation or imagination and it is possible that the subtlety of Aristotle—his clear-cut definitions and theories—should have attracted young Spenser more than the imaginative philosophy and the poetic visions of Plato,

[1] *Journal of English and Germanic Philology*, Vol. XXV. p. 284.
[2] Hales' Memoir, p. xx.

## 12   PLATONIC IDEAS IN SPENSER

though a few of his ideas of love and poetic art crept into the *Shepheards Calender*. A Latin verse-letter[1] to Harvey written by Spenser about the time of the publication of the *Shepheards Calender* (i.e., as early as 1579), reveals the hold which Aristotle's doctrine of the mean had on the young poet. Moral allegories were very common in Spenser's days; yet the allegorising in the *Faerie Queene* of the moral virtues as discussed and illustrated in Aristotle's *Ethics,* shows the power of the spell cast by Aristotle's intellectual subtlety over the early years of Spenser's life and authorship. For, though published in 1590, the *Faerie Queene,* Part I had been composed at least in part by 1580 when it was submitted to Harvey for his criticism.[2] As for Part II of the poem, though it was published in 1595-1596, portions of it had probably been written before 1580 when Spenser was sojourning with the Sidneys and the Dudleys.[3] At any rate, the scheme of

---

[1] Translated into English by Richard Wilton and printed in Grosart's Edition of Spenser's Works, Vol. I. Appendix, p. 433.

[2] Spenser in his letter dated the 10th April, 1580 wishes Gabriel Harvey to return the poem with his 'long-expected judgment'.

[3] See Hales' opinion about the date of composition of *Epithalamion Thamesis,* now part of Bk. IV. of the

## INTRODUCTION 13

the whole epic must have been conceived[1] some time before 1580, and in Part II the poet was merely working out this scheme which shows how he valued superficial symmetry more than deeper organic unity in a work of art like the *Faerie Queene*. For instance, the design of the epic is controlled by the enumeration of virtues in the *Nicomachean Ethics*. 'The Faery Queene kept her annuall feaste xii days: uppon which xii severall dayes, the occasions of the xii severall adventures hapned, which, being undertaken by xii severall knights, are in these xii books severally handled and discoursed.'[2] Arthur, as the type of perfection (Magnificence), is to appear once in each of the twelve books. The smaller episodes are based on the descriptions of the moral virtues and their subdivisions.[3] Though Spenser's Letter to Raleigh was dated January 23, 1589 (or 1590, according to the New Style), the scheme of the epic which found expression in it had already materialised to a considerable extent before 1580 when Spenser was less than thirty. This letter,

*Faerie Queene*, in his Memoir, p. xxvii. Spenser had a habit of re-writing his poems.
[1] Spenser's statement reported in Bryskett's book (written before 1582) referred to above, also supports this view.
[2] See Chapter III. *post.*    [3] See Chapter I. *post.*

apart from its express declaration that Spenser was following Aristotle's ethical speculations, also reveals the poet's early love of symmetry and intellectual subtlety.

This earlier period of the poet's life is to be marked off from his later years of contemplative depth to which belongs the composition of the *Amoretti,* the *Epithalamion* and the *Fowre Hymnes* (*circ.* 1593-96) which run over with the finest Platonic (and also Neo-Platonic) conceptions without any tinge of Aristotle's influence and the tone of which is definitely against the spirit of Aristotle's cold intellectualism. There are some works of the intermediate period, viz., the *Teares of the Muses* and *Colin Clout* written in 1591, which contain no noticeable Aristotelian ideas but only a few ordinary Platonic thoughts. But the idealism of Plato was so congenial to the spirit of Spenser that even in one of his earlier productions, viz., Part I of the *Faerie Queene* (apart from the October Eclogue of the *Shepheards Calender*) Platonic conceptions[1] appear prominently side by side with Aristotelian ideas. Yet this debt to Plato was not expressly acknowledged in the poet's Letter to Raleigh, simply because Aristotle

[1] See Chapters I. and II. *post.*

# INTRODUCTION 15

loomed large before his eyes in his youth, and it looks as if the poet was not himself aware of it.

It is to be noted that as Spenser advanced in years, he not only shook off the influence of Aristotle's theories,—of his logical and subtle intellect—and came more and more under the influence of Plato, but the Platonic ideas in his composition became more and more tinged with Neo-Platonism. Miss Winstanley in a note to her *Introduction* to the *Fowre Hymnes* says, 'Spenser's works seem to show two main periods of Platonic influence, one early (*Shepheards Calender* and *Faerie Queene*, Bk. I) which consists of Platonism pure and simple and the other later (*Faerie Queene*, Bk. VII and *Amoretti*) in which the Platonism is largely mixed with Neo-Platonism.' Though Miss Winstanley makes no mention of them, Books II. and III. of the *Faerie Queene* (published in 1590 along with Book I. of this poem) must, besides Book I. and the *Shepheards Calender,* be included in the early period; for there are only Platonic ideas in them without any infusion of Neo-Platonism and with clear marks of Aristotle's influence. During the next few years of Spenser's authorship, almost no trace is found in his work of Plato's or even of Aristotle's influence. There are only faint

## 16  PLATONIC IDEAS IN SPENSER

impressions of Plato's ideas in the *Teares of the Muses*[1] published in 1591 in a volume entitled *Complaints*. Stray ideas of Plato also occur in *Colin Clout* written in 1591 and published in 1598.[2] Part II of the *Faerie Queene* which was published in 1595-96 but the scheme of which had been conceived many years ago, has more Aristotelian ideas in it than Platonic. The period that followed was, in the words of Miss Winstanley, the later period of Platonic influence tinged largely with Neo-Platonism and it covered the composition of the *Fowre Hymnes* besides the two other poems mentioned by her. Spenser's works of this period illustrate his obligation especially to the Italian treatises of Neo-Platonists like Pico, Bembo and Castiglione who elaborated the Neo-Platonic ideas as interpreted by Ficinus and expressed Neo-Platonic mysticism in graceful literary forms. The change of Spenser's literary taste in the direction of Italian Neo-Platonism was probably the effect of a change of taste in con-

---

[1] e.g., in the speech of Urania in which knowledge is described as capable of uplifting the human soul through intermediate stages, like dialectic in Plato, to a vision of the Highest Being.

[2] Love inspiring poetic efforts, beauty encouraging man to enlarge his ' kynd ', cosmogonic love helping creation—all these are Platonic ideas.

## INTRODUCTION 17

temporary England and its increasing appetite for things Italian. At Cambridge the love of Italian authors succeeded the rage for classical studies which was the vogue in Spenser's time.[1]

The composition of Spenser's sonnet-cycle was distributed over the period 1592-95. Though in the Petrarchan vein, the *Amoretti* show traces of Italian Neo-Platonism as shaped in their sonnets by French sonneteers like Ronsard, Du Bellay and Pontus de Thyard. The composition of the *Epithalamion* synchronises with that of the last sonnets of this cycle, though the former is full of purely Platonic ideas and celebrates the successful issue of the courtship the varying course of which is described in the *Amoretti*.[2] The Hymns to Heavenly Beauty and Heavenly Love were composed during Spenser's stay in England in 1595-96 and were published in 1596 with the other two Hymns which, Spenser says in his Dedication, had already been in circulation. The influence of Italian Neo-Platonism (especially as in Benivieni) is most marked in these four poems and they are

---

[1] This is pointedly described in one of the letters of Harvey. See *Spenser* in the E.M.L. Series, p. 25.

[2] There are, however, scholars who think that some of the sonnets at least were originally composed in honour of Lady Carey.
See *Modern Language Review*, Vol. V. p. 274.

## 18  PLATONIC IDEAS IN SPENSER

also the finest productions of Spenser in point of melody, artistic beauty and maturity of thought. The 'greener times' to which Spenser refers the composition of the first two Hymns could not possibly have been the date of composition of the *Shepheards Calender,* as Herford suggests;[1] for there is a clear distinction between the purely Platonic conceptions of love in the October Eclogue taken directly from the *Symposium* and the Neo-Platonic aesthetic theories derived from Ficinus and his followers like Pico and Castiglione and noticeable in these Hymns. These must have been the outcome of the poet's subsequent studies. The influence of Bruno, if it is a reality, must point to the same conclusion. The Hymns to Beauty and Love must have been actually written not very long before the two last Hymns. This inference is supported by the similarity of their diction which is flawless throughout and also by the fact that a unity of conception and design runs through the four Hymns and the two later Hymns continue the topic dealt with in the earlier ones,[2] taking it up just where it had been left by them. It is, of course, possible, as Miss Winstanley

---

[1] See p. xviii of the *Introduction* to Herford's Edition of the *Shepheards Calender*.
[2] See chapter V. *post*.

## INTRODUCTION 19

suggests, that 'the two earlier *Hymnes* belonged to a period of erotic poetry but were altered and amended for publication'.[1] But this period could not have long preceded the date of composition of the last two Hymns, though some difference between the two sets is clearly felt. This consists in (1) the Christian[2] colouring and (2) the Christian interpretation given to Neo-Platonic mysticism, which are the special features of the last two Hymns.

Neo-Platonism in Spenser has received a separate treatment and the chapters dealing with it form the second division of the present volume.

---

[1] See p. lxxii of her *Introduction* to the *Fowre Hymnes*.
[2] See *Modern Language Notes*, Vol. XLV. p. 327.

# PLATONISM

## CHAPTER I

### BLENDING OF THE IDEAS OF PLATO AND ARISTOTLE—TEMPERANCE

SOME critics look upon Spenser's conception and treatment of the virtue of Temperance as strictly Aristotelian and the second book of the *Faerie Queene* as an exposition of the Aristotelian doctrine of self-control as set forth in the *Nicomachean Ethics*.[1] Miss Winstanley in her *Introduction* to Bk. II. traces its moral ideas chiefly to the *Ethics,* though she admits Plato's influence in a few cases. There can be no doubt about Spenser's obligation to Aristotle in the second book of his poem, but critics have mostly overlooked the part played by Plato's philosophy in it. On the other hand, Harrison has traced, though very briefly, all the ethical ideas of Bk. II. to Plato.[2]

According to Aristotle, virtues are concerned with actions and the study of ethics is not speculative but practical. Aristotle has therefore

---

[1] *Modern Philology*, Vol. XVI. p. 251.
[2] *Platonism in English Poetry*, p. 12.

# TEMPERANCE 21

classified virtues and vices and subjected them all to a detailed examination. As the philosopher of right conduct, he has preached the avoidance of the extremes and the pursuit of the mean. His ideas are practical and easy to comprehend, but Plato's contemplative mood feels no interest in details and concrete rules and Plato tries to go beyond the separate virtues and vices as manifested in action and conduct and to find out their common source in the human soul. It is man's inner life that forms the subject-matter of Plato's enquiry and the one thing which Plato emphasizes so strongly in his dialogues[1] is the unity of moral life or the unity of virtue. The *Republic* also records Plato's enquiry into human virtue which, according to his doctrine of unity of virtue, comprehends all such attributes as temperance, courage, justice and wisdom.[2] Plato maintains that there is a close analogy between virtue in man and virtue in the State and discovers in man's inner being three principles corresponding to the three different classes of citizens of the State,—the rulers (in Plato's language, 'guardians'), the soldiers and the labouring classes.[3] These principles are reason,

---

[1] See the *Protagoras*, 329.
[2] *Republic*, Bk. IV. 442.   [3] *Republic*, Bk. IV. 440-441.

passion and appetite. When the two other classes do their respective duties properly under the guidance of the guardians, the State enjoys peace resulting in the greatest happiness of its members. Similarly, so long as the two other principles of the soul do their respective duties under the guidance and direction of reason, there is health or harmony in man's life. This is the state of Temperance which is not the virtue of any particular part or principle of the soul, but is the result of the agreement among all as to who should be their controller and guide. It may also be called the state of justice in the soul, as justice in Plato consists in a man's doing his own duty and harmony in the soul is possible only when the different principles confine themselves within the spheres of their respective duties and do not overstep their boundaries. Discord ensues when a subordinate principle—passion or appetite—tries to arrogate to itself the function of reason and it manifests itself as anger or concupiscence. As Plato puts it, there is a disease in the soul corresponding to every disease in the State—Timocracy, Oligarchy or Democracy.[1] Plato considers harmony to be the normal condition of the soul and every form

---

[1] *Republic*, Bk. VIII.

## TEMPERANCE

of discord to be a disease and a vice. Hence harmony in the soul may be called the condition precedent to the growth of every virtue in it,—it may even be regarded as virtue itself the unity of which he is never weary of emphasizing. 'The just man does not permit the several elements within him to interfere with one another . . . he sets in order his own inner life, and is his own master and his own law, and at peace with himself'.[1] 'Must not injustice be a strife which arises among the three principles—a meddlesomeness and interference?' This comprehensive idea—so characteristically Hellenic—is expressed through a different imagery in the *Phaedrus*. The tripartite division of the soul and the conception of balance or harmony underlie the figure of the two winged horses and a charioteer driving them.[2] The charioteer stands for reason, while the horses typify anger and appetite.

It must be admitted that there has been a curious blending of the ethical ideas of Plato and Aristotle in Bk. II. For Spenser, obviously, a critical and discriminating study of their systems was impossible, and the Aristotelian mean and the Platonic

---

[1] *Republic*, Bk. IV. 443.  [2] *Phaedrus*, 246, 253.

harmony, Aristotle's classification of virtues and Plato's theory of their unity were mixed up in this poem. The result is to be seen not merely in the presence of Platonic ideas side by side with Aristotelian but also, on occasions, in the misfitting of one class of ideas into the other. At times, Spenser interprets the same incidents and characters both in the manner of Aristotle and of Plato, and below the cut-and-dried Aristotelian diagram often flows the undercurrent of Platonic thought. The design of the poem seems to have been determined by Aristotle's classification of the objects of self-control and the episodes appear to illustrate the different kinds of intemperance as conceived by Aristotle. In Bk. III. ch. XIII. of his *Ethics,* Aristotle says, 'The habits of perfected self-mastery and entire absence of self-control have for their object-matter such pleasures as brutes also share in . . . they are touch and taste'.[1] Subsequently Aristotle merges taste in touch. Anger and things like money, gain and honour are also regarded as objects of self-control in Aristotle. Vice (κακία), incontinence (ἀκρασία) and brutality (θηριότης) are the three kinds of moral defect to be avoided.[2]

---

[1] *Ethics,* Bk. III. ch. XIII.   [2] *Ethics,* Bk. VII. ch. I.

## TEMPERANCE

The adventures of Guyon are devised in conformity with this classification. His first and greatest enemy is Acrasia (symbolising 'touch' of Aristotle's *Ethics*) whom he undertakes to subdue in the very first canto of Bk. II. Furor and Pyrochles represent anger and Mammon and Philotime stand for wealth (or gain) and ambition (or 'honour', as in Aristotle) respectively. The monsters who besiege the castle of Alma represent vice and Maleger brutality. But strict adherence to the *Ethics* has been rendered impossible by the influence of Plato. According to Aristotle, 'Temperance will apply to bodily pleasures only (i.e., the pleasures of touch), but not to all even of these'.[1] Thus the word 'incontinent' is not applicable, in an absolute sense, to those who transgress the limits of right reason but are not given to sensuality; 'but we qualify the word by saying that they are incontinent in respect of money or gain or honour or angry passion. We do not speak of them as incontinent in an absolute sense, because they are different and are called incontinent only by *analogy*'.[2] Miss Winstanley is not, therefore, correct in stating that according to Aristotle absolute incontinence

[1] *Ethics*, Bk. III. ch. XIII.  [2] *Ethics*, Bk. VII. ch. VI.

'applies to anger' as much as to sensual passions ;[1] for Aristotle looks upon licentiousness as the only object of self-control strictly so called. But in Bk. II. Pyrochles, Furor and Mammon are as formidable enemies of Guyon as Acrasia, and the poet's view is clear that anger and greed for money are as much to be avoided as incontinence in respect of bodily pleasures. Importance is attached to anger through Guyon's adventures in the very first six cantos of the poem which are directed against types of irascibility, because Plato recognises passion (i.e. anger) and appetite as the two equally powerful enemies of reason in the *Phaedrus* as well as in the *Republic*. In spite of the fact that the vice of appetite is dealt with in the latter part of Bk. II., Acrasia is the most powerful conception in the poem ; and though Spenser is indebted to Tasso for his marvellous description of the witch and her bower, in all their languid and sensuous beauty, there is sufficient indication of the poet's inner conviction that licentiousness is more reprehensible than anger. In this, however, is again noticeable the influence of Aristotle who says, 'Passion follows reason in a sense, but desire does not. Desire is

---

[1] *Introduction* to Bk. II. p. lxiv.

## TEMPERANCE

therefore more disgraceful, for the man of incontinent temper is in a sense the servant of reason, but the other is the servant of desire and not of reason.'[1] Again, 'Incontinence which is due to desire is more unjust than the incontinence which is due to angry passion; for there is nothing of wantonness in angry passion'.

The underlying conception of every one of the principal characters in Bk. II. manifests the influence of Plato's philosophy of harmony, though, at the same time, the actual moral attribute it represents and its expression in overt action may have been suggested by Aristotle's scheme in the *Ethics*. Miss Winstanley says that Pyrochles and Cymochles are both examples of the Aristotelian extreme of excess in courage, i.e., foolhardiness, while Braggadocchio stands for another extreme, viz., cowardice and Guyon represents the mean or true courage. While this is generally true (the objection to this view will be discussed later), it is to be noted that Pyrochles is not represented merely as a dare-devil fighter, but also as one who is himself suffering from extreme mental anguish. The character of Pyrochles as drawn by Spenser shows clearly the influence of the

---

[1] *Ethics*, Bk. VII. ch. VII.

Platonic theory of discord. Pyrochles stands for the vehemence of anger, but the poet emphasizes the turmoil in his soul—his inward burning—more strongly than the violence of his overt action or his foolhardiness. Pyrochles' rashness and readiness to fight are previously announced by his servant Atin. When he appears on the scene, he commences the fight without even stopping to greet Guyon. He fights rashly and is defeated. Guyon then tells him not to mind the defeat in this fight, as a more terrible fight is going on in his soul.

> ' Fly, O Pyrochles! fly the dreadfull warre
> That in thy selfe thy lesser partes do move;
> Outrageous *anger*, and woe-working *jarre*,
> Direfull *impatience, and hart-murdring love* : '
> (C. V. st. 16).

In Plato anger, as already pointed out, is a disturbance of the soul which is due to the overthrow of the rule of reason. That the intemperance of Pyrochles is an inward discord of the soul is manifest from the exclamations of the giant warrior when he throws himself into the river to quench his burning sensation :—

> ' I burne, I burne, I burne! . . . . . .
> O! how I burne with implacable fyre;
> Yet nought can quench mine *inly flaming syde* '—
> (C. VI. st. 44)

## TEMPERANCE

The overthrow of reason from the position of the ruler of the inner life is evidenced by an absence of discrimination from the mind of the foolhardy man. Knowledge and discrimination are essential parts of courage according to the teachings of both Plato and Aristotle. Says Aristotle, '*Experience and skill* in the various particulars is thought to be a species of courage. Hence it was that Socrates himself conceived courage to be knowledge'. . . . . 'By reason of their *skill* they (soldiers) are better able than any others to inflict without suffering themselves, because they are able to use their arms'.[1] Again, 'one who is in a condition of incontinence either does not possess an opinion, or possesses it in a sense in which possession, as we said, does not mean *knowledge* but merely the repetition of phrases'.[2] 'Actions in accordance with virtues are not, e.g., justly or temperately performed because they are in themselves just or temperate. It is necessary that the agent at the time of performing them should satisfy certain conditions, i.e., in the first place, that he should *know* what he is doing, secondly that he should deliberately choose to do it'.[3] In

---

[1] *Ethics*, Bk. III. ch. XI.  [2] *Ethics*, Bk. VII. ch. V.
[3] *Ethics*, Bk. II. ch. IV.

Plato's *Laches,* Socrates says, 'He (Nicias) appears to mean that courage is a sort of *wisdom*'. The same view about the connection between courage and knowledge or discrimination is to be met with in the *Protagoras*[1]. Pyrochles starts fighting in a violent but *tactless* manner and the *skill* of Guyon soon brings him down on his knees, begging for his life.[2] Some purely Aristotelian traits also are noticeable in the character of Pyrochles. The *Ethics* states, 'He is brave who withstands and fears and is bold in respect of right objects, from a right motive, in a right manner and at right times.'[3] 'Nobleness is the motive from which the brave man withstands things-fearful'. Guyon's motive in undertaking his adventures is the destruction of the Bower of Bliss. This is a worthy motive; but Pyrochles has no such motive for seeking Occasion. 'All in blood and spoil is his delight'.

Cymochles has been wrongly put in the same

---

[1] *Protagoras*, 359-361.
[2] The possibility of cowardly conduct on the part of a foolhardy man is suggested by Aristotle. He says, 'Most foolhardy people are cowards at heart, for although they exhibit a foolhardy spirit where they safely can, they refuse to face real terrors'.
[3] *Ethics*, Bk. III. ch. X.

category as his brother Pyrochles.[1] He is sunk, when he first appears in Canto V.[2], in the mire of sensuality or incontinence and Atin reprimands him as a 'womanish weake knight'.[3] He is lulled to sleep in a shady bower by Phaedria with song (and wine) even after he has been roused by Atin to help his brother. As a knight he has, of course, to draw the sword now and then; but he fights with Guyon because he suspects his rivalry in love.[4] Though his bravery is referred to pointedly,[5] rashness is not his defect. He does not seek Occasion like Pyrochles, nor is he so full of violent and angry feelings as Pyrochles always is. The latter tries to rob Guyon of his armour even after he has been knocked senseless in the fight.[6] Pyrochles was 'inflamed with rage' when he saw Guyon lying senseless[7] and he 'gan his brother fiers reply'[8] when Cymochles was arguing with the Palmer about the merits of Guyon. Pyrochles *violently and suddenly* attacked Arthur without giving him any time for preparation, but Cymochles remained silent till he was roused to

---

[1] See *Modern Philology*, Vol. XVI. p. 246 and L. Winstanley's *Introduction* to Bk. II. p. lxiii.
[2] St. 32–34.     [3] C. V. st. 36.
[4] C. VI. st. 28.     [5] C. V. st. 26.
[6] C. VIII. st. 14, 17.     [7] C. VIII. st. 12.
[8] C. VIII. st. 15.

action by the injury inflicted on his brother by Arthur.[1] According to the Platonic imagery, Cymochles' soul is marked by the ascendancy of concupiscence over reason and this explains the difference between Cymochles and Pyrochles who is never ensnared by sensuality. Cymochles is the embodiment of licentiousness and as 'incontinence assumes sometimes the form of impetuosity, and at other times that of weakness,'[2] Cymochles is both violent (i.e., impetuous) and supine.

Like Pyrochles, Cymochles is represented, in conformity with the theories of both Plato and Aristotle, as wanting in skill and knowledge. Being grossly sensual, he too is a tactless fighter. Both the brothers are defeated and killed by Arthur who in Bk. II. represents Temperance and is therefore depicted as a skilful fighter possessing in an abundant measure tact and wisdom so essential to courage. Furor is an abstraction and as such is a symbol of the Platonic conception of discord in human soul caused by the supremacy of passion over reason. Though he is a violent fighter and a 'man of mickle might'[3], he has no skill and no discernment of his opponent's strength,

[1] C. VIII. st. 33.  [2] *Ethics*, Bk. VII. ch. VIII.
[3] C. IV. st. 7.

## TEMPERANCE

because knowledge which is the basis of courage cannot dwell in a discordant soul. As he had 'no governaunce to guyde' his strength, his 'force was vaine', his blows were wide of the mark, he often hurt himself unawares, his 'reason, blent through passion, nought descryde' and he was like a 'blindfold Bull'.[1] Furor represents what Aristotle would call the madness[2] of incontinence in anger. 'Fits of anger and the desires of sensual pleasures and some such things do unmistakably produce a change in the condition of the body, and in some cases actually cause *madness*'.

Mordant was a high-souled knight,—the 'gentlest Knight'—till he fell a victim to licentiousness (Acrasia). His degradation also is represented by Spenser as an inner phenomenon, for sensuality according to Plato is a disturbance of the soul's harmony caused by the ascendancy of concupiscence over reason. His 'frailtie' comes from the flesh.[3] The change effected in Mordant by sensuality affects his inner life and intellectual powers and is thus described by his wife Amavia:—

> '—so transformed from his former skill,
> That me he knew not, nether his owne ill '.
> (C. I. st. 54).

[1] C. IV. st. 7.   [2] *Ethics*, Bk. VII. ch. V.
[3] C. I. st. 52.

## 34  PLATONIC IDEAS IN SPENSER

While this is the Platonic analysis of the character of the fallen Mordant, Spenser also interprets his tragedy in the manner of Aristotle. Temperance in Aristotle consists in following the golden mean, and Mordant ought to have pursued a *via media* between total abstinence and excess. The Aristotelian doctrine is referred to in the following lines :—

> '—temperaunce . . . with golden squire
> Betwixt them both can measure out a meane ;
> Nether to melt in pleasures whott desyre,
> Nor frye in hartlesse griefe and doleful tene ' :

Plato speaks of music and gymnastics[1] as the means of promoting harmony in the moral life of man,—music having the effect of soothing down animal passions and gymnastics of counteracting the inner tendency to inaction due to appetite and an immoderate exercise of the rational faculty. Thus the remedies for the diseases of the soul are all internal and are suggested by his comprehensive theory that the health of the soul depends on a balance of its three elements—reason, passion and appetite. Aristotle, on the other hand, looks upon a moral defect like intemperance as a physio-

---

[1] *Republic*, Bk. III. 410.

logical or a nervous disorder. He says, 'Fits of anger and the desires of sensual pleasures and some such things do unmistakably produce a change in the condition of the body'.[1] Again, 'If vice may be compared to such a disease as dropsy or consumption, incontinence may be compared to epilepsy, the one being a chronic, the other an intermittent depravity.'[2] Aristotle also likens intemperance to slumber. 'It is clear, then, that we must regard incontinent people as being in much the same condition as people who are *asleep* or mad or intoxicated. ... If it be asked how the incontinent person is delivered from ignorance and restored to knowledge, it may be answered that the process is the same as in the case of one who is intoxicated or asleep. It is not peculiar to the condition of incontinence, and the proper authorities upon it are the physiologists.'[3] Therefore in Acrasia's Bower, Verdant, one of the victims of the enchantress, is found in deep slumber. But Spenser follows Plato exclusively in dealing with Mordant, and Amavia brings back her husband, degraded by intemperance or the ascendancy of concupiscence over

---

[1] *Ethics*, Bk. VII. ch. V.    [2] *Ibid*. ch. IX.
[3] *Ibid*. ch. V.

reason in Acrasia's Bower, to his normal condition by a wise direction[1] of his inner life. She says :—

> '—through wise *handling* and *faire governaunce*
> I him recured to a better will,
> Purged from drugs of fowle *intemperaunce*':

The conception of Phedon's character is mainly Aristotelian, though his episode is imitated from Ariosto.[2] Phedon is a victim of the angry passion but he feels remorse for his hasty actions. His vengeance seems just at first sight and, according to Aristotle, the passionate man seems to follow reason in a way.[3] Yet the influence of Plato's theory is not wanting. Phedon is intemperate and Spenser lays special stress on the internal jar produced in him by his passion. The violence of this discord almost drives him mad and is represented by the attacks of Furor, instigated by Occasion, on him.[4] The Palmer's reprimand to Phedon shows a correct diagnosis of his disease and this is strictly Platonic,[5] revealing as it does, the overthrow of reason by the 'affections'. The nature of Phedon's intemperance is further sug-

---

[1] This corresponds to music or harmony as defined by Plato. See *Republic*, Bk. III. 401–403.
[2] See *Orlando Furioso*, IV. V.
[3] *Ethics*, Bk. VII. ch. VII. and L. Winstanley's *Introduction* to Bk. II. of the *Faerie Queene*, p. lxiv.
[4] C. IV. st. 33.  [5] C. IV. st. 34.

## TEMPERANCE

gested by the traits of his enemy Furor. He is not a tangible or material being that can be easily destroyed but is a symbol of passion or mental fury which cannot be removed without the reinstatement of harmony in the soul[1].

The castle of Alma is an obvious allegory of the Platonic doctrine of harmony in the soul[2] and no influence of the *Ethics* of Aristotle can here be suggested, as there can be no suggestion of Platonic influence in the case of the Palmer, Braggadocchio or Amavia.[3] Alma is the rational soul and the smooth working of her castle, secured through the obedience of her agents or servants, symbolises the Platonic theory of Temperance or the agreement amongst the faculties of man to obey one of them as their ruler. Spenser has not, however, strictly followed Plato's three-fold division. The number of those who work obediently under Alma is not given, but certainly

---

[1] C. IV. st. 10.  [2] C. XI. st. 2.
[3] See L. Winstanley's *Introduction* where the sources of the first two characters in Aristotle's *Ethics* are given. As for Amavia, she can be called a coward in the Aristotelian sense. Aristotle says, 'It is the act, not of a courageous person, but rather of a coward, to fly from poverty or love, or anything that is painful, by death.' (*Ethics*, Bk III. ch. XI.) She can also be called 'effeminate', which means 'unable to hold out against pain.' (*Ethics*, Bk. VII. ch. VIII.)

it is more than two. The description of the siege of the castle contains much foreign element and, of the twelve 'troupes' employed in it, the seven stationed at the gate symbolise the Seven Deadly Sins, while those directed against the five bulwarks stand for the five senses. With all this mediaeval imagery, the underlying Platonic idea is clearly discernible that 'no war is so fierce as that of the passions with the soul.'

> ' What warre so cruel, or what siege so sore,
> As that which strong *affections doe apply*
> *Against the forte of reason evermore*,
> To bring the sowle into captivity ? '
> (C. XI. st. 1).

The episode of the three sisters illustrates how Spenser made a confusion of Platonic and Aristotelian ideas and formed an awkward combination of them. Most critics look upon the sisters as an illustration of the Aristotelian theory of the extremes and the mean and the argument to the second canto by Spenser[1] himself confirms their view. Miss Winstanley says that Medina, the mean, stands for Aristotle's gentleness, 'for gentleness is treated in a special way by Aristotle,

---

[1] Doubts have, however, been expressed about Spenser's authorship of the arguments to the cantos.

## TEMPERANCE 39

being given four extremes, and the same occurs with Medina who has not only her sisters opposed to her but also the lovers of her sisters."[1] The extremes or opposites of gentleness are irascibility, quick temper, sullenness and sternness and Miss Winstanley thinks that these attributes are symbolised in Sansloy, Perissa, Elissa and Hudibras respectively. It seems, however, that Spenser was wrong in putting an Aristotelian interpretation on the story of the three sisters and that he has been responsible for misleading many of his critics, including Miss Winstanley. As Kitchen observes, 'Here the poet deviates from the philosopher. His defect, the frowning Elissa, is not merely too little of the quality of which "excess", the gay Perissa, is too much; but each of them is a definite and independent obliquity. The one is too fond of pleasure, the other is too morose and gloomy.'[2] Excess and defect always imply a difference of degree, not of kind. It is, however, clear from the poet's characterisation of Elissa and Perissa that they are intended to be types of two separate vices—anger and sensuality.[3]

---

[1] *Introduction* to Bk. II. p. lxi.
[2] Kitchin's *Introduction* to Bk. II. of the *Faerie Queene*, p. ix.
[3] Canto II. st. 35–37.

Perissa is described as 'quite contrary to her sisters kynd'. 'Wine and meats', 'pleasure and delight', 'excess' and 'love' constitute the atmosphere in which she lives and moves. Her lover Sansloy joins in her 'looseness' and 'leawd parts'. This picture is fundamentally different from the other in which 'lowring browes' and 'frowning' are so clearly marked. Medina is dressed 'in modest guize' and is 'a sober sad and comely courteous Dame'. She is found sitting between her two sisters and controlling them.[1] The function of control is allotted by Plato to reason, but nowhere by Aristotle to the mean. When Medina's control is strong, there is peace and harmony in the family; but whenever it is slackened, the two other sisters create disturbance by inciting their lovers to fight. It is thus clear that these three sisters signify the tripartite division of the soul in Plato, though they seem to stand for the Aristotelian extremes and the mean.

The two knights Hudibras and Sansloy also represent the same vices as their paramours; they do not symbolise the excess and the defect of the same vice, as urged by Miss Winstanley. In Hudibras are to be noticed all the elements which

[1] C. II. st. 38.

anger or passion comprises in Plato. He has taken part in many rash adventures; yet he is not really courageous—'not so good of deeds, as great of name',—because courage depends on obedience to reason, while Hudibras' reason is 'with foolehardize overran'.[1] He is 'more huge in strength then wise in workes'. Sansloy is introduced as an assaulter of Una and he is 'to lawlesse lust encouraged'.[2] These two knights thus typify anger and appetite.

The Platonic analysis of the soul into three distinct principles seems also to have suggested the relation among the three characters Pyrochles, Cymochles and Arthur or Guyon. Reason in Plato has to stand the combined onslaught of both passion and appetite, and Pyrochles and Cymochles 'both attonce him (i.e., Arthur) charge on either syde.'[3] But reason is strong enough to cope with both its enemies. Hence Arthur deals 'blowes on *either* side'[4] till the two brothers are laid low on the ground. Similarly Guyon repels both Hudibras and Sansloy when attacked by them simultaneously from two sides. The description of this fight as 'a triple warre with

[1] C. II. st. 17.   [2] C. II. st. 18.
[3] C. VIII. st. 35.   [4] C. VIII. st. 41.

triple enmitee,[1] is an Aristotelian reminiscence; for, according to the *Ethics,* the extremes are opposed to each other and also to the mean and Hudibras and Sansloy were fighting with each other before attacking Guyon.

Guyon's character, as distinct from his relation with Pyrochles and Cymochles, also bears traces of the influence of both Plato and Aristotle. Guyon is not only the Aristotelian mean[2]; he also represents the Platonic Temperance. He is the mean between the foolhardiness of Pyrochles and the cowardice of Braggadocchio and his courage, unlike that of his two enemies, depends on his knowledge and skill as defined in the *Ethics*.[3] Aristotle's influence is also seen in his moral condition in the cave of Mammon and in the island of Phaedria where he feels the temptation and yet resists it and triumphs over it.[4] But Spenser also interprets his character as the effect of harmony in his soul. The Redcrosse Knight recognises his enemy to be Guyon by the latter's

[1] C. II. st. 26.
[2] It may be pointed out that Guyon learns the fundamental conception of Temperance in the Castle of Medina.
[3] Bk. III. ch. XI.
[4] A temperate person is not absolutely insensible to temptation.

# TEMPERANCE

'goodly governaunce'.[1] The very first lines describing the bearing of the Knight of Temperance run thus :—

> ' His carriage was full comely and upright ;
> His countenance demure and *temperate* '.
> (C. I. st. 6).

When Redcrosse and Guyon discover their mistake which had made them into enemies ready to fight, Guyon turns 'his earnest unto game, through goodly handling and wise *temperaunce*.'[2] Medina, when she welcomes Guyon to her castle, meets him

> ' Fayre marching forth in *honorable* wize '.
> (C. II. st. 14).

The feeling of order is conveyed even through the movements of the knight's charger.[3]

Maleger is Aristotle's brutality. It is difficult to ascertain whether he also stands for any Platonic conception of vice. Undoubtedly some marks of the unjust man or the tyrant as delineated in the *Republic*[4] are noticeable in him. These are his extreme truculence, his unscrupulous character as indicated by his cowardly methods of fighting and his poisonous darts,[5] his impotence and his

---

[1] C. I. st. 29.   [2] C. I. st. 31.
[3] C. I. st. 7. See also Harrison's *Platonism in English Poetry*, p. 25.
[4] Bk. IX. 571–575.   [5] C. XI. st. 21.

impatience (symbolised in the hags). The unjust man is the opposite of the temperate and hence Arthur, in place of Guyon, is Maleger's opponent. But the comprehensiveness and profoundness of the Platonic conception are wanting in the character of Maleger.

Verdant, the young lover of Acrasia, is a concrete illustration of the theory of Aristotle that an incontinent person is like one who is asleep, mad or intoxicated.[1] He awakes as soon as the effect of incontinence on him is removed by the arrest of Acrasia and profits by the 'counsell sage' of the Palmer. The metamorphosis of the beasts into human beings was undoubtedly suggested by the story of Circe but the underlying idea that the souls of men deprived of their rational faculty by vice, passed into the bodies of lower animals, was possibly derived from Plato's *Phaedo*.[2]

The allegorical treatment of the Platonic analysis of the soul is not original in Spenser who was anticipated on this point by Tasso[3] whom Spenser regarded as his master in many respects. The

---

[1] *Ethics*, Bk. VII. ch. V.   [2] See chapter II. *post*.
[3] Spenser's description of the siege of the Castle of Alma, again, is supposed to have influenced T. Tomkis' play *Lingua* (1607). See Vol. XLII. of *Modern Language Notes*, p. 150.

interpretation of the *Jerusalem Delivered* by Tasso himself, as embodied in the chapter entitled 'Allegory of the poem', describes its subject-matter as the 'rebellion which the concupiscent and ireful powers do make with the Reason'. It also mentions Plato's analysis of the soul. This interpretation has however been regarded as an after-thought of the poet and as a sop to the Inquisition.

## CHAPTER II

### CHASTITY

CHASTITY, the subject of the third book of the *Faerie Queene*, is identified by some critics with the Aristotelian virtue of 'shame' (*Verecundia*). But Aristotle himself says that a sense of shame is 'more like an emotion than a moral state' and that it may be defined as a kind of 'fear of ignominy' and is 'in a sense corporeal'.[1] Chastity is regarded by others as but another aspect of Continence (ἐγκράτεια) or Temperance (σωφροσύνη) dealt with in Book II. Dean Church, for instance, says of Book III : 'It is a repetition of the ideas of the latter part of the Book II, with a heroine Britomart in place of the Knight, Sir Guyon'. But Chastity as expounded by Spenser is something different from temperance, Aristotelian and Platonic. The Aristotelian conception is almost akin to the virtue of abstinence, for the mean has to steer clear of the extremes of excess and defect of pleasure, especially the pleasure of touch. Thus it is a negative ideal Platonic temperance is a

[1] *Ethics*, Bk. IV. ch. XV.

state of harmony in the soul,—that state in which its different parts do their respective duties in implicit obedience to the dictates of reason. No doubt, temperance itself is a great virtue; yet Plato holds that this state of the soul is a condition precedent to the growth of other virtues in it. Chastity is to be looked upon as one of such virtues and it constitutes a clear advance on both the above conceptions, viz., harmony in the soul and avoidance of the extremes in the enjoyment of pleasure. It is a positive conception and really means noble love between man and woman. It demonstrates Spenser's humanism which prefers the glow of life to the chill of moral austerity. Dowden says, 'There is no Chastity, Spenser would assure us, so incapable of stain as the heroic love of a magnanimous woman'.[1] Britomart's love of Artegall is the main theme of the third book. It is undoubtedly based on temperance, because no noble love is possible in any one whose soul is in tumult and is the battle-ground of conflicting principles. At the same time, it is something more than temperance. The difference between mere temperance and love was apparent to Plato himself, as is clear from Socrates' recanta-

---

[1] *Spenser, the Poet and Teacher.*

tion after his first speech in the *Phaedrus* praising the rigid austerity of the non-lover. In his second speech he puts the lover far above the non-lover and the madness or frenzy of love is applauded as far nobler than the calm of temperance, because every great and noble thing has at its root love or frenzy as its generating cause.[1]

The Platonic idea of love has to be appreciated with reference to the state of society in Athens in the days of Plato. In Greek cities of those times, love between youths was very common. For a youth to be without a lover was looked upon as strange and also objectionable. The older of the pair was called the lover and the younger the beloved or 'listener'. In civilised Greece youthful attachment was often deliberately encouraged owing to considerations of military training. It was the duty of the lover to train up his beloved in feats of arms and the *lovers fought side by side, endangering their lives* for the sake of their country. In the *Symposium* Plato himself refers to this in the speech of Pausanias. In some states this type of attachment between youths was sanctioned by law, while in others it was prohibited;

---

[1] *Phaedrus*, 244.

## CHASTITY

for tyrants generally feared combinations of young men as tending to undermine their power.[1]

Probably in ancient Greece love between youths was a relic of more barbarous times and grosser social practices. Jowett in his *Introduction* to the *Symposium* says, 'It is impossible to deny that some of the best and greatest of the Greeks indulged in attachments which Plato in the *Laws,* no less than the universal opinion of Christendom, has stigmatised as unnatural'. The darker side of love between young men was obvious to Plato and in the *Charmides* and the *Lysis* it is made sufficiently clear that physical beauty was often the cause of the formation of friendship amongst young men. Plato tried to use this type of love or friendship as a stepping-stone to the higher notion of love based on virtue. As Jowett says, 'He is conscious that the highest and noblest things in the world are not easily severed from the sensual desires or may even be regarded as a spiritualised form of them'. He enunciates the higher love on the analogy of vulgar love. The latter affords vulgar pleasures or the pleasures of the senses, while the former, according to Plato, leads to the pleasures of the intellect or of the soul. In the case of the former,

[1] See the speech of Pausanias in the *Symposium*, 182.

the beloved derives virtue and wisdom from the lover, leading to the elevation of his inner nature. 'Evil is the vulgar lover who loves the body rather than the soul . . . and therefore when the bloom of youth which he was desiring is over, he takes wing and flies away, in spite of all his words and promises; whereas the love of the noble disposition is life-long.' Plato explains later what this 'love of the noble disposition' means and says, 'These two customs, one the love of youth, and the other the practice of Philosophy and virtue in general, ought to meet in one, and then the beloved may honourably indulge the lover. For when the lover and beloved come together, having each of them a law, and the lover on his part is ready to confer any favour that he rightly can on his gracious loving one, and the other is ready to yield any compliance that he rightly can to him who is to make him wise and good; the one capable of communicating wisdom and virtue, the other seeking after knowledge, and making his object education and wisdom; when the two laws of love are fulfilled and meet in one, then and then only, may the beloved yield with honour to the lover.'[1]

[1] Pausanias' speech in the *Symposium*, 184.

# CHASTITY

By an extension of this idea of virtuous love between man and man, Plato arrives at the conception of the love of Absolute Beauty in the *Symposium*[1] and of True Being in the *Phaedrus*.[2] In all this discussion about true love or spiritual love, not a word is said by Plato about any ideal of man's relation with woman. From the context it is clear that Plato has not been thinking of the true and noble affection which man feels for woman. Neither in the *Symposium* nor in the *Phaedrus,* nor even in the *Republic* where this philosopher has been making experiments in social reconstruction and political organization, shrinking from nothing in his search for justice—not even from community of wives,—is there any suggestion about the possibility of true love or community of feelings and ideals between man and woman. In Plato true love (or, in his own language, 'chaste' love) means friendship between man and man for purposes of education and moral elevation and 'unchaste' or vulgar love means love between such parties based on physical attraction and reminiscent of unnatural vice. Mention is made of woman only with reference to vulgar love. Pausanias says, 'The love who is

---

[1] *Symposium*, 211.   [2] *Phaedrus*, 247.

the offspring of the Common Aphrodite is essentially common, and has no discrimination, being such as the meaner sort of men feel, and is apt to be of *women* as well as of youths, and is of the body rather than of the soul'. In connection with his doctrine of generation or birth in beauty, Plato mentions woman once more.[1] Plato thus brings in woman only where love of the body is concerned ; but Plato's favourite theory is that connection with sense renders the soul gross so as to impede its heavenward flight. Thus the leading philosopher of Greece and its apostle of spiritual love recognises woman's power for evil but not her immense power for good over man.

The ideal of Chastity[2] in the third book of the *Faerie Queene,* though remotely suggested by Plato, is really a complex conception—a combination of Platonism, Chivalric traditions and Christian ideas. The conception of spiritual love between soul and soul or between man and man is derived from Plato, the application of this idea to the attraction of man for woman is due to the tradition

[1] See the well-known speech of Diotima in the *Symposium*, 208.
[2] The word *Chastity* appears first in connection with moral virtues in Bullein's *Dialogue* vs. *the Fever Pestilence*—1st Ed., 1564. See *Modern Philology*, Vol. III. p. 377.

## CHASTITY

of chivalry and the ideal of wedlock[1] which is pointed out as the consummation of true love, is the final reward of lovers like Britomart and Artegall, Florimell and Marinell and Scudamore and Amoret and is celebrated in the *Epithalamion*, is taken from the teachings of the Reformed Christian Church which proclaimed the impossibility of the practice of rigid celibacy. Combinations of different ideals which had flourished under divergent circumstances at different times, are not unusual; for it was the influence of chivalry combined with the ethics of the Christian Church that led Dante to body forth his ideal love in a lovely woman.[2]

The legend of Chastity as a whole is rather formless, but its loosely-connected episodes are based on the distinction between the two kinds of love—vulgar and spiritual—as described by Plato. The characters that apprehend only the beauty of the body are Malecasta, Argante the giantess, the witch's son, Proteus, the fisherman, Malbecco and Paridell. But Britomart, Amoret and Florimell are attracted by the beauty of the spirit or of the soul. The episodes arise out of the clash between these two sets of characters.

---

[1] e.g., in the *Faerie Queene*, Bk. III. C. III. st. 3.
[2] *Contemporary Review*, Vol. LVIII. p. 412.

Florimell who loves Marinell falls into the power of beastly creatures like Proteus, the fisherman and the witch's son and whenever she succeeds in escaping from the clutches of one, ill luck throws her into the grasp of another. Amoret, the chaste lady attached to Scudamore, is a victim to the enchantments of Busirane who is vanquished by Britomart, the Knight of Chastity. Malecasta, with all her beauty and refinement, is a type of sensual desire and is held up by Spenser as a warning to chaste ladies[1] and Britomart is seen in her true colours when she is with Malecasta in her castle.

Britomart is the champion knight of the third book, and Spenser has tried to illustrate in her character Plato's theory that noble love is attracted only by the beauty of the soul and of high ideals. Britomart falls in love with Artegall on seeing his reflection on the mirror and what strikes her in this reflection is his 'manly face'[2] and heroic and honourable bearing rather than his physical beauty.

> 'Portly his person was, and much increast
> Through his *Heroicke grace and honorable gest.*'
> (C. II. st. 24).

The description of Artegall by Redcrosse as one

[1] C. I. st. 48–50.  [2] C. II. st. 24.

## CHASTITY

of the greatest and most courageous knights in the fairy-land fills Britomart with joy.[1] Merlin calls him 'the prowest knight that ever was' and inspires Britomart with a prophecy of the great glory to which her love was likely to lead Artegall. He would fight for her country[2] against 'the powre of forreine paynims which invade thy land' and would be the founder of a famous line[3] of rulers. Britomart herself subsequently

> 'Beheld the lovely face of Artegall
> Tempred with *sternesse* and stout *majestie*—'
> (Bk. IV. C. VI. st. 26).

It was thus the vision of some superior excellence in Artegall that captivated her heart. The nobility and purity of her love becomes evident when compared with the passion of other princesses mentioned by Britomart's nurse Glauce,—the Arabian Myrrhe, Biblis and Pasiphaë.[4]

The speech of Phaedrus in the *Symposium* attributes an inspiring power to noble love. 'The principle which ought to be the guide of men who would nobly live—that principle, I say, neither kindred, nor honour, nor wealth, nor any other motive is able to implant so well as love . . . .

[1] C. II. st. 9–11.   [2] C. III. st. 27.
[3] C. III. st. 29.   [4] C. II. st. 41.

Who would desert his beloved or fail him in the hour of danger? The veriest coward would become an inspired hero, equal to the bravest, at such a time : Love would inspire him. That courage which, as Homer says, the god breathes into the soul of heroes, Love of himself infuses into the lover'. This is why noble love is differentiated by Plato from temperance which is a form of abstinence and is thus a passive virtue. Love in Spenser not only stirs up 'th' Heroes high intents'[1] or 'does alwaies bring forth[2] bounteous deeds', but also drives away vices like idleness and 'ungentlenesse'.[3]

> ' For love is lord of truth and loialtie,
> Lifting himselfe out of the lowly dust '—
> (*H. L.* st. 26).

In his study of Spenser's conception of chastity, Harrison says that 'in him the teaching of the beauty of moral ideas came to fruition in ennobling the conception of human life by an appreciation of the true beauty of woman's inner nature, her womanhood, and by a conception of love that placed its source in the reverent adoration of this spiritual beauty'.[4] 'With this vision of the res-

---
[1] C. III. st. 2.　　　　[2] C. I. st. 49.
[3] C. V. st. 1–2.
[4] *Platonism in English Poetry*, p. 31, 38.

# CHASTITY

plendent beauty of chastity begins Artegall's love for Britomart'. While this view is true so far as it goes, it does not comprehend the whole range of Spenser's idea of Chastity in Book III., nor does it give the real meaning of the allegory. 'The thirde booke of the *Faerie Queene'* is described by Spenser as 'contayning the Legend of Britomartis, or of Chastity,' as the first two books are called Legends of Redcrosse and Guyon respectively. The Letter to Raleigh also refers to 'a Lady Knight in whome I picture Chastity' and states that Scudamore, the lover of Amoret, having failed to rescue her from the prison of the sensual Busirane, Britomart, as the champion of Chastity, undertakes the task in fulfilling which she suppresses the 'Maske of Cupid'. Artegall's love of Britomart finds no place in Book III. and he sees her for the first time and falls in love with her in Canto VI. of Book IV. Artegall, moreover, represents justice, not chastity and is the champion of Book V. Though Spenser values the beauty of woman's inner nature or true womanhood (as celebrated in the *Epithalamion,* for instance) and represents beastly creatures like the witch's son and Proteus as enjoying merely physical beauty, it is not Artegall's love of this inner beauty of woman (Britomart) that is allegorised as the Legend of Chastity in Bk. III. Again, the constituents of the true beauty of woman's inner nature—her womanhood, as Dr. Harrison puts it—e.g., modesty, sweetness and grace do not all appear so prominently in Britomart as in Amoret and Florimell, though sensuality is the abhorrence of all. To refer to Artegall's appreciation of Britomart's spiritual beauty or womanhood as the meaning of the Legend of Chastity is thus misleading. Chastity in Book III. refers mainly to the moral attribute of Britomart, not of Artegall; and it has been described in clear outline by the poet at the very beginning of the Legend. This moral attribute consists more of mental energy and strength of will than of sweetness, amiability or grace. Her inborn courage was heightened by a training in arms. Hers was a fighting, dynamic[1] personality and though she was a young girl unaccustomed to the ways of the world, love prompted her to renounce ease, comfort and seclusion and urged her on to high endeavours to

'—seeke an unknowne paramoure,
From the world's end, through many a bitter stowre—'
(C. III. st. 3.)

[1] 'Her life must be a life of arduous action and sustained endeavour', says Aubrey de Vere.

She is the personification of the power, resourcefulness and inspiration of noble love, and chastity in Spenser is but another name for this noble love.

Mere possession of inner beauty and spiritual grace or appreciation of such moral qualities in others, did not by itself constitute Plato's view of chastity or love which was adopted by the Renaissance. Its glowing ideal conceived of love as an urge of the soul which impelled people to seek for union with their beloved and to raise themselves thereby to a higher plane. Love, Spenser says,

> ' —to the highest and the worthiest
> Lifteth it up that els would lowly fall :
> It lettes not fall, it lettes it not to rest ; '
> (C. V. st. 2).

This view is responsible for the selection of Britomart as the champion of chastity in preference to Florimell, Amoret and Belphoebe. Though all of them stand on the same plane of moral purity as Britomart, none can compare with her in the urge of her soul which finds expression in her heroic efforts, her unceasing endeavour to meet her beloved. Having no lover, Belphoebe stands apart ; hers is an almost aimless life. Florimell 'is the fairest wight alive'[1] and 'stedfast chastitie and vertue rare' are 'the goodly ornaments' of her beauty. Amoret is trained in female graces or 'trew feminitee' in the Garden of Adonis and she sits in the very lap of womanhood in the Temple of Venus.[2] Renwick aptly marks off 'Britomart and Belphoebe and Amoret, different conceptions of chastity—that which depends on strength and faithfulness, that which is a noble fastidiousness removed from common frailty, and that which is a natural attribute of womanly character'.[3] Florimell and Amoret are very similar in their womanly character. Their love is indeed firm and constant, but it is not anything different from the ordinary human passion which is not based on a spiritual bond and has no inspiring powers. They are really types of passive female virtue and grace, without any very distinct personality of their own (though Florimell seems to have greater energy and initiative than Amoret and the contrast between Florimell and false Florimell, as Miss Winstanley points out, is suggested by the Platonic distinction between the

---

[1] C. V. st. 5.
[2] Bk. III. C. VI. st. 51 and Bk. IV. C.X. st. 52.
[3] *Edmund Spenser*, p. 159.

beauty which is of the body only and the beauty which is of both body and soul).[1] Chastity and noble love, however, postulate in Spenser an inner urge of high aspirations based on mental energy and strength of will. Lack of these virtues makes them inferior to Britomart and renders them liable to attacks by types of sensuality like the witch's son, Proteus and Busirane. The 'Maske of Cupid' and the mural pictures in the house of Busirane where Amoret was imprisoned, indicate the quarter whence she may expect danger and difficulty. But Britomart who possesses in an abundant measure the virtues which the other two ladies lack, is so secure in her chastity that no danger can assail her. Her noble love is really the magic spear which gives her victory everywhere. As Miss Winstanley points out, Guyon in Bk. II. feels temptations and overcomes them but Britomart, protected by her noble love, feels none.

Arthur alone can compare with Britomart in noble love. Having seen the beauty of the Fairy Queen Gloriana in a dream, he devoted himself to a prolonged search for her and, like Britomart, shrank from no danger or difficulty in his quest. The beauty which inspired Arthur to glorious

[1] *Introduction* to Bk. II. p. lvi.

deeds was, as Guyon says in Bk. II., the beauty of Gloriana's mind,

> 'That is, her bounty, and imperiall powre,
> Thousand times fairer than her mortall hew,'—
> (Bk. II. C. IX. st. 3).

Scudamore who had won Amoret from the Temple of Venus, after defeating as many as twenty valiant Knights, belonged to a different type of lovers distinctly lower than Britomart and Arthur. He secured Amoret with the help of the shield of love which was the shield of Cupid. But Cupid and Uranian Venus are different, and not being a votary of noble love as described by Plato, Scudamore was lacking in the 'Heroës high intents'. He was therefore incapable of entertaining high hopes and Britomart found him grovelling on the ground and groaning in despair.[1] Busirane was a more powerful votary of Cupid whose conquests were depicted on the arras in his house,[2] and that is why Scudamore was unable to pass through the flames which the magician had kindled. But Britomart having been inspired by a higher and nobler type of love, the flames gave way before her and the graceful Amoret was easily rescued from the clutches of vulgar passion by her superior power of chastity.

[1] C. XI. st. 9–17.   [2] C. XI. st. 27–46.

Spenser develops in his Hymns the Neo-Platonic theory of the connection between the soul and the body, the formative energy of the soul and its influence on physical beauty and the effect of moral virtue on human body.[1] In the third book of the *Faerie Queene* he anticipates these ideas and associates ugliness with moral turpitude, especially with sensuality. Persons whom Plato would regard as unchaste,—those that enjoy only physical beauty—are all ugly in appearance. Such are the fisherman, the witch's son, Proteus and Argante. True and lasting beauty is the exclusive possession of the chaste or the morally good, e.g., Florimell, Amoret and Britomart. Those that are inordinately unchaste and excessively intemperate suffer the utmost physical degradation and are changed into beasts, which means the total extinction of reason. Spenser here seems to follow Plato who says that the souls of 'men who have followed after gluttony and wantonness and drunkenness and have had no thought of avoiding them, would pass into asses and animals of that sort'.[2] Those who are not excessively sensual are not indeed subjected to the extreme penalty of transformation into the likeness of beasts; yet

---

[1] See chapter V. *post.*     [2] See the *Phaedo*, 81.

they have to undergo some kind of physical and intellectual degradation. The witch's son and the forester who gave chase to Florimell, belong to this class. They have only a faint glimmering of reason and their appearance is uncouth and almost indistinguishable from that of beasts.[1]

Spenser follows Plato in describing the effect of the beauty of chaste women on the beholder. Plato has tried to explain it through the fanciful figure of the chariot drawn by two winged horses. When a beautiful woman is in sight, one of the horses is full of the 'ticklings of desire'; but when the charioteer sees her, 'his memory is carried to the true beauty and beholds her in company with Modesty, set in her holy place. And when he sees her, he is afraid and falls back in *adoration*.'[2] Another effect of beauty is that the beholder is *amazed* and almost *benumbed* at the sight of it. Says Socrates, 'He who has become corrupted is not easily carried out of this world to the sight of absolute beauty in the other. . . . But he whose initiation is recent, and who has been the spectator of many glories in the other world, is *amazed* when he sees any one having a God-like face or form

---
[1] Cf. the beasts in the Bower of Bliss in Bk. II.
[2] *Phaedrus*, 254.

## CHASTITY

... and at first a *shudder runs through him'*. In Spenser Britomart is the type of chastity and when, in a fight with Artegall, her helmet is destroyed, the knight is taken aback at the sight of her amazing beauty. His arm is benumbed with fear, his sword drops to the ground and he himself kneels down before her in adoration.[1] On another occasion, a similar awe-inspiring effect was produced on the guests assembled in the Castle of Malbecco when Britomart had to put off her armour. They were seized with 'suddein great affright' at the sight of her beauty and it seemed as if they were absorbed

'In contemplation of divinitee:'[2]

But the beauty of Hellenore, the wife of Malbecco, produced no such effect on them. The report of her beauty had travelled far and wide and had been the subject-matter of conversation amongst them just before she appeared. Yet, the poet says, she only 'shewd her selfe in all a gentle courteous Dame'.[3] Such is the difference between the beauty of a chaste lady and the false glamour of a vicious woman. Spenser has modelled the love-story of Artegall and Britomart

[1] Bk. IV. C. VI. st. 21, 22.   [2] C. IX. st. 24.
[3] C. IX. st. 26.

on Ariosto's episode of Bradamante and Ruggiero. Britomart is a romantic heroine with many of her features taken from Tasso's Clorinda and Ariosto's Bradamante—a full-blooded woman undergoing the physical perturbations of passionate love as well as its moral agonies, such as jealousy. But the influence of Plato is responsible for the difference between the two stories of Ariosto and Spenser in respect of their tone and outlook and for 'the contrast of the passionate love of beauty revealed in Spenser's poem with the superficial delights of love as explained in Ariosto'.[1]

According to Plato, it is only the virtuous man retaining a memory of his ante-natal vision of Absolute Beauty who appreciates true beauty in this world and worships it. But Spenser goes further and says that beauty has the power of extorting reverence from every man, virtuous or vicious, and striking him with awe. The son of the witch was a grossly sensual creature; yet when he first saw Florimell in his mother's cottage, he felt prompted to worship her.[2] Similarly, when the fisherman awoke and saw Florimell on his boat, he was entranced and dazzled with the

[1] Harrison's *Platonism in English Poetry*, p. 39.
[2] C. VII. st. 11.

# CHASTITY

glorious vision of her beauty. As the poet puts it, it seemed as if 'some extasye assotted had his sense, or dazed was his eye', though this experience of his was very transitory.[1]

The story of Malbecco and Hellenore may indeed be looked upon as a Rabelaisian episode. It also contains veiled and irreverent sneers in the manner of Boccaccio against established institutions and cherished ideas current in contemporary England. But it may, in addition, be looked upon as an illustration of disgust at mere physical love as expressed in Plato. One of the marks of this kind of attraction is the jealousy of the lover who is always afraid lest somebody else should carry off the object of his enjoyment and is therefore unwilling to let a third person approach his beloved. The infatuation becomes specially strong when the disparity in age between the lover and the beloved is very great. Socrates says, 'The lover is not only unlike his beloved, but he forces himself upon him. For he is *old and his love is young,* and neither day nor night will he leave him, if he can help. But what pleasure or consolation can the beloved be receiving all this time? Must he not feel the extremity

[1] C. VIII. st. 22, 25.

of disgust when he looks at an old shrivelled face? .... Moreover he is *jealously watched and guarded against everything and everybody*'.[1] In Spenser the old husband Malbecco shut up his young and fair wife Hellenore in his castle and he had to be repeatedly requested by Paridell and Britomart before he allowed her to come out and dine with them. Spenser's description[2] of the condition of the wife shows how miserable she was and it is no wonder that she eloped with Paridell.

In an article in the *Modern Philology,*[3] De Moss reads Helen into Hellenore and Paris into Paridell.[4] He also tries to trace the moral of the story to Aristotle's *Ethics.*[5] According to Aristotle, chastity is a form of friendship which includes the relationship between husband and wife and is based on the equality of the parties. Hellenore is 'unequal' to Malbecco in age and differs from him in mentality and this disparity is responsible for her unchastity.

Spenser's ideal of chastity, as embodied in

[1] *Phaedrus*, 240.   [2] C. IX. st. 5.
[3] Vol. XVI. p. 258.
[4] But Paridell in the poem traces his descent from Paris. See C. IX. st. 35–37.
[5] *Ethics*, Bk. VIII. Ch. IX.

Britomart, consists of noble love between man and woman. Britomart, however, is to be contrasted with Florimell and Amoret on the one hand and, on the other, with another image of chastity, viz., Belphoebe who personifies an ideal which is not Platonic but Mediaeval.[1] Her birth even was free from the taint of passion. She and Amoret were twins but the difference in their training was responsible for the subsequent difference between the two sisters. She was taken away by Phebe or Diana to be 'upbrought in perfect Maydenhead,' while Venus undertook to train up Amoret in 'goodly womanhed' in the garden of Adonis. Belphoebe loves spiritual beauty which is a sublime abstraction and not a concrete reality. She makes light of worldly joy and pleasure and her austerity and aloofness mar the harmony of her character. This becomes patent when she is compared with Britomart. It was the Middle Ages that held Belphoebe's ideal of chastity very high; but even the Middle Ages looked upon it as almost beyond the reach of ordinary mortals and believed that chaste people of this world could possess only a very faint copy of this ethereal virtue, just as earthly beauty is but

[1] *Journal of English and Germanic Philology*, Vol. XVI. p. 70.

a reflection of heavenly beauty.[1] But Belphoebe's character derives some tinge from that of the classical Diana,[2] the virgin huntress, after whom she is named. It also borrows something from the Mediaeval institution of warrior-saints or fighting ascetics like the Templars and the Hospitallers.

Britomart, as contrasted with Belphoebe, is a product of the spirit of the Renaissance which Spenser had imbibed in an abundant measure; and though Spenser's appreciation of the good points of the Mediaeval ideal is beyond all doubt, his delineation of the two characters like Britomart and Belphoebe side by side shows clearly to which his sympathy leans,—whether to the spirit of the Middle Ages or to the culture of the Renaissance.

[1] C. V. st. 52.
[2] See Spenser's Letter to Raleigh.

## CHAPTER III
### TRUTH

EARLIER critics of Bk. I. of the *Faerie Queene* were mainly concerned with tracing its historical allegory and its broad religious significance. They looked upon it chiefly as shadowing forth the struggle between Catholicism and Protestantism in England together with the historical personages who took part in it and, secondly, as representing man's struggle after purity and his triumph over sin under the guidance of 'gospel truth'.[1] But they missed the impress of Plato's philosophy on it, though they noted the personification of the Aristotelian idea of perfection in Arthur in consequence of Spenser's mention of it in his Letter to Raleigh. But in this very letter Spenser clearly says that he derives from Aristotle all the virtues of which his principal knights are the champions. As Aristotle's *Ethics* makes no mention of Holiness, the source of this virtue has now become a matter of controversy the possibility of which had never been foreseen.

[1] Kitchin's *Introduction* to the *Faerie Queene*, Bk. I. p. xiii.

## 72  PLATONIC IDEAS IN SPENSER

Jusserand, on noting the want of correspondence between Spenser's Letter to Raleigh and the *Faerie Queene*, infers that the Aristotelian studies of the poet's earlier years were overlaid with his later readings in moral treatises based on Aristotle or Plato but actually written by less noted authors like Piccolomini, La Primaudaye and Bryskett and that, as a result of the confusion of ideas that ensued, he mentioned Aristotle as his source, while he was in fact following these authors. As illustrations, Jusserand mentions that the number 12 as the total of Aristotle's moral virtues mentioned in Spenser's Letter to Raleigh, occurs only in Piccolomini and Bryskett[1] and that Aristotle's list of ethical virtues is not the same as Spenser's. Holiness which is not to be found in the *Ethics*, is mentioned in a French work by La Primaudaye published in 1577.[2] This writer was well-known in England as a Platonist, and this indicates that if Holiness has to be traced to a source outside Christianity, it cannot be Aristotle; it is more likely to be Plato.

Kitchin too is of the same opinion as Jusserand about Spenser's obligation to Aristotle in Books I. and II., though he expresses himself differently.

---

[1] Aristotle in fact has a total of 13.
[2] *Modern Philology*, Vol. III. p. 381.

# TRUTH 73

He says, 'Spenser . . . is obliged to break away from the plan he laid down for himself in his well-known Letter to Sir Walter Raleigh. To have worked out the twelve Books as representing "the twelve moral virtues", each with its own knight and its own adventures, would have demanded a far narrower treatment of these two opening Books. Instead of ranging over the whole extent of human life and interests as they do, pourtraying Holiness and Temperance, we should have had the adventures of the liberal soul struggling against extravagance or stinginess, or the brave man attacked by temptations of rashness or of cowardice. The genius of the poet happily delivered him from his own bonds'.[1]

De Moss, a critic of Jusserand's theory, takes his stand on the express declaration of his debt to Aristotle by Spenser in his well-known Letter and, in reply to Jusserand, points out that Spenser was not ignorant of the real total (13) of Aristotle's private moral virtues; for, though he speaks of 'the twelve private[2] morall vertues, as

---

[1] *Introduction* to Bk. II. p. vi.
[2] Percival says this total number (i.e., 12) of the private virtues, but not their names, is also found in the title of an old French book on the Laws of Arms, dated **1488** (*Introduction* to the *Faerie Queene*, Bk. I. p. xi).

Aristotle hath devised' in the first paragraph of his Letter to Raleigh, he adds to them magnificence which, as the last sentence of the second paragraph shows, is not included in 'the xii other vertues'. De Moss also makes a desperate attempt to trace Holiness to the *Ethics* and identifies it with Aristotle's magnanimity or high-mindedness.[1] He suggests no reason why Spenser should have changed the designation of the virtue from magnanimity to Holiness, a word unknown to Aristotle, but sets forth the grounds for his view that Redcrosse stands for magnanimity. The poet's description of Redcrosse—of his love of glory, sense of honour, etc.—in his opinion, fits in with the characterisation of the high-minded man in Aristotle. This argument is not very convincing. De Moss also attaches great importance to the incidents in Bk. I. and the adventures of its champion knight and he thinks that these adventures are modelled on the detailed description of magnanimity in the *Ethics*. But the enemy of Redcrosse is not meanmindedness, the Aristotelian opposite of magnanimity, but a dragon or evil. The most important adventures of Redcrosse comprise encounters against

[1] *Modern Philology*, Vol. XVI. p. 32.

## TRUTH

Error, Pride (Orgoglio) and Atheism (Sansfoy), and his succour and inspiration come from the House of Holiness. Unlike the high-minded man, he misjudges his own abilities and has to take Prince Arthur's help. 'The discipline in humility to which he is subjected is very foreign to Greek thought' and is also opposed to the spirit of the virtue called magnanimity.

De Moss's theory is also in clear conflict with the scheme of the poem as set forth in one of the passages of Spenser's Letter to Raleigh which, strangely enough, is quoted and relied on by this critic himself. It runs thus : 'So *in the person of Prince Arthure I sette forth magnificence in particular;* which vertue, for that (according to Aristotle and the rest) it is the perfection of all the rest, and conteineth in it them all, therefore in the whole course I mention the deedes of Arthure applyable to that vertue, which I write of in that booke. But of the xii other vertues, I make xii other Knights the patrones'. Probably the poet inadvertently puts 'magnificence' for 'magnanimity'.[1] If there be no inadvertence, then by 'magnificence' Spenser means what is

[1] *Modern Philology*, Vol. III. p. 382.

commonly called 'magnanimity'.[1] For it is magnanimity, if not justice,[2] that answers to the description contained in the passage quoted above,—'it is the perfection of all the rest'. Magnificence has a special meaning in the *Ethics*— it is a virtue 'having for its object-matter Wealth; but it does not . . . . extend to all transactions in respect of Wealth, but only applies to such as are expensive'.[3] On the other hand, 'the very name of Great-mindedness implies that great things are its object-matter' and 'whatever is great in *each virtue* would seem to belong to the great-minded'. Again, Aristotle says, 'This virtue, then, of Great-mindedness seems to be a kind of ornament of *all the other virtues,* in that it makes them better, and cannot *be without them*; and for this reason it is a hard matter to be really and truly Great-minded'. Thus, if magnanimity, high-mindedness or great-mindedness comprehends the other virtues, Arthur fittingly becomes the type of this perfect virtue and not of magnificence, for Spenser's object is 'to pourtraict in Arthure, before he was king, the image of a brave

---

[1] See Percival's *Introduction* to the *Faerie Queene*, Bk. I. p. lvi.
[2] *Ibid.* p. xii.
[3] *Ethics*, Bk. IV. Ch. III.

knight, perfected in the twelve private morall vertues, as Aristotle hath devised'. Arthur's position in the scheme of the *Faerie Queene* supports this view. He takes part in the chief adventure of each book and brings help to its champion knight. Hence his activities vary and illustrate all the ethical virtues of Aristotle. Spenser remarks in his Letter, 'In the whole course I mention the deedes of Arthure applyable to that vertue, which I write of in that booke'. As pointed out by Hurd, Arthur's part in each book is *essential,* though not *principal.* 'In each book he appears as an auxiliary (and not as principal), and inferior, for the time, to the knight whom he helps; but in the 12 books together he appears, at last, as superior to them all, by uniting the whole circle of the virtues in himself'. If Arthur is great-mindedness, Redcrosse also cannot stand for this perfect virtue, as De Moss tries to establish. Spenser also specifically says that the *twelve* other champion Knights are types of virtues *other than* 'magnificence' or great-mindedness. It is clear from an examination of the poem and from a comparison between Arthur and Redcrosse that they do not symbolise the same virtue. Redcrosse appears only in one book and therefore cannot compare with Arthur who, according to the scheme, must appear in every book and take part in the adventure of every knight as necessity for his help arises. Again, if both Arthur and Redcrosse were intended to typify the same virtue, their activities should have been similar in nature. The high-minded man, says Aristotle, 'is capable of conferring benefits but ashamed of receiving them, as in the one case he feels his superiority and in the other his inferiority'. The Redcrosse Knight is not, like Arthur, a warrior imagining himself to be superior to others, disdaining their help and showering his favour or patronage on an admiring circle of followers. His weakness is obvious in the deception successfully practised on him by Duessa, his defeat by Orgoglio, his correction in the House of Holiness and his rescue by Arthur. There is thus overwhelming evidence to show that Arthur, and not Redcrosse, stands for the Aristotelian virtue of Perfection or magnanimity and that Redcrosse, the vanquisher of the dragon or Sin, must represent some other virtue less comprehensive than it.[1] Though the Aristotelian scheme has been applied to the treatment of Holiness in Bk. I. (Sansfoy and

---

[1] See *Journal of English and Germanic Philology*, Vol. XXII. p. 3 where Padelford disagrees with De Moss.

# TRUTH

Corceca being its extremes of defect and excess respectively and Redcrosse the mean), there is no virtue in Aristotle so profound in its import and its moral significance, so boundless in its hope, so deep in its fervour as Purity.

As Plato is more profound and more transcendental than Aristotle, there is a natural temptation in critics to seek for the source of Holiness in Plato. Holiness occurs in three dialogues of Plato, but without any clear or specific meaning. In the *Euthyphro*[1] Holiness is defined as 'that part of Justice which attends to the gods, as there is the other part of Justice which attends to men'. In the *Laws*[2] it is said that 'he who would be dear to God must, as far as is possible, be like Him and such as He is. Wherefore the temperate man is the friend of God, for he is like Him; and the intemperate man is unlike Him, and different from Him and unjust'. This 'temperate' or just man is later mentioned as a holy man. 'The unholy do only waste their much service upon the Gods, but when offered by any holy man, such service is most acceptable to them'.[3] In the *Protagoras*[4] emphasis is laid on the unity of virtue which is variously called Temperance,

---
[1] *Euthyphro*, 12.  [2] *Laws*, IV. 716.
[3] *Laws*, IV. 716–17.  [4] *Protagoras*, 329.

## 80  PLATONIC IDEAS IN SPENSER

Holiness and Justice. It would thus appear that Plato means by Holiness his comprehensive virtue of Justice. Jowett remarks, 'The subject (Holiness) is not elsewhere (i.e., besides the three dialogues named above) resumed by Plato, nor is holiness reckoned among the virtues in his later dialogues. Probably, if we may judge from the indications which he has supplied in the *Protagoras* and the *Euthyphro,* he regarded holiness as a part of Justice and thought, therefore, that it did not require further discussion apart from the virtue under which it was included'.[1] Miss Winstanley suggests that Spenser's Holiness corresponds to courage (ἀνδρεία) in the dialogues of Plato who means by it the essential quality of manliness or moral courage. It is the foundation of all other virtues and is thus equivalent to Justice. Aristotle also mentions ἀνδρεία, but as he means by it merely courage[2] in war, it cannot be the source of Spenser's Holiness.

Justice, as meant by Holiness in Plato, is not explained in the Dialogues where the latter expression occurs, but is discussed in the *Phaedrus,* the *Phaedo* and the *Republic.* The conception of justice is based on the Platonic doctrine of Ideas

---
[1] 'Holiness' in the *Index* to the Dialogues.
[2] *Introduction* to Bk. II. p. liii.

according to which there is a supreme Reality called Truth (or Beauty) which can be perceived by the human mind only after it has gone through a long stage of preparation. The *Phaedrus* portrays the vision[1] of this Reality as it appeared to the soul in its ante-natal state. The *Phaedo* goes a step further and indicates what kind of preparation will enable the human soul to have a glimpse of it. Both the *Phaedrus* and the *Phaedo* emphasise what is called the absolute purity of Truth or its transcendental nature and state that the human mind or soul can have a vision of it only when it is free from the impression of sense or attains to purity, holiness or justice. The means, according to the *Phaedo,* consists in removing the soul's tendency to sense-perception and in the concentration of its powers on itself, rendering it intellectual, holy or just. Says Socrates, 'The soul is only able to view real *existence* through the bars of a prison, and not in her own nature. She is wallowing in the mire of all ignorance; and Philosophy, seeing the terrible nature of her confinement, and that the captive through desire is led to conspire in her own captivity, received and gently counselled her, and wanted to release her,

---

[1] *Phaedrus*, 247.

pointing out to her that the eye is full of deceit, and also the ear and the other senses and, persuading her to retire from them in all but the necessary use of them, and to be *gathered up and collected into herself*, and to trust only to herself and her own *intuitions of absolute existence, and mistrust* that which comes to her through others and is subjected to vicissitude'.[1] Ordinary knowledge is derived from sense-perception and sometimes from generalisation from experience gathered through it; but the knowledge of Truth, the final Reality as conceived by Plato, can be acquired only through the intuitive effort of the mind after it has been purged of sense-impression. This effort has been called dialectic in the *Republic*. It has its basis in a previous training in abstract sciences like music, arithmetic, geometry and astronomy which, in varying proportions, embody the activity of pure intellect free from the impressions of sense. 'When all these studies reach the point of intercommunion and connection with one another, and come to be considered in their mutual affinities, then, I think, but not till then, will the pursuit of them have a value for our objects; otherwise there

[1] *Phaedo*, 83.

# TRUTH

is no profit in them' 'And so, Glaucon . . . we have at last arrived at the hymn of dialectic. This is that strain which is of the intellect only, but which the faculty of sight will nevertheless be found to imitate; for sight, as you may remember, was imagined by us after a while to behold the real animals and stars, and last of all the sun himself. And so with dialectic; when a person starts on the *discovery of the absolute* by the light of *reason only, and without any assistance of sense,* and perseveres until by pure intelligence he arrives at the perception of the absolute good, he at last finds himself at the end of the intellectual world, as in the case of sight at the end of the visible'.[1] Intellectual training to the entire exclusion of sense-knowledge is insisted on more expressly in Neo-Platonism. Plotinus classifies virtues[2] into political, cathartic and theoretic, and he defines cathartic virtues as those 'that pertain to reason alone, withdrawing from other things to itself, throwing aside the *instruments of sense* as vain.' The Alexandrian philosopher asserts that the practice of these (i.e., cathartic) virtues leads man to Holiness (or 'justice' in the language of Plato) and prepares

---

[1] *Republic,* VII. 532.
[2] See Plotinus' *Enneads,* II. ii. tr. T. Taylor.

him for union with Truth. He follows Plato in describing the process to be adopted. 'We must enter deep into ourselves, and leaving behind the objects of corporeal sight, no longer look back after any of the accustomed spectacles of sense . . . . On the contrary, neglecting all these as unequal to the task, and excluding them entirely from our view, having now closed the corporeal eye, we must stir up and assume a purer eye within, which all men possess, but which is alone used by a few'. Thus according to both Plato and Plotinus, Holiness is purified Intellect communing with Truth or Beauty. It has been suggested that Redcrosse symbolises this Platonic or Neo-Platonic conception of Holiness, that Una is the ultimate Reality or Truth and that the adventures of the knight emblem the overcoming of obstacles to the realisation of Truth. Says Harrison, 'The underlying idea taught by Spenser in the first book is that *holiness* is a state of the soul in which wisdom or *truth* can be seen and loved in and for its beauty'. Again, 'In the *Phaedo,* the function of philosophy is explained to lie in the exercise by the soul of this power of spiritual *contemplation of true existence.* In Spenser this conception is further illustrated by the part which the schooling, received by the

Redcrosse Knight on the Mount of Contemplation, played in the perfection of his *mental* vision'.[1] Miss Winstanley remarks, 'In the *Phaedrus* Plato explains that it is possible by the practice of virtue so to train and instruct the soul that it becomes conscious of *wisdom and truth* as visible things and can conceive them in their native beauty as they really are. It is *this state* of mind which Spenser understands as Holiness'.[2] Percival refers to Plato's discussion in the *Timaeus* (87), *Gorgias* (508) and *Theaetetus* (176) on the connection between love, beauty and happiness and asks, 'Is it difficult to trace, in this doctrine, the main action of the first book of the *Faerie Queene*?' The answer is given by him in these words : 'Una's is this Beauty and Goodness : the *Redcrosse Knight's is this love* : Duessa's is this Ugliness and Evil, whose companionship leads to the Misery of Orgoglio's dungeon'.[3] The opinions of these distinguished scholars seem to be open to criticism, because Spenser's Holiness is a *moral* virtue quite different from *intellectual* perfection which is the ideal of Plato. Undoubtedly Plato, in his plea

[1] *Platonism in English Poetry*, p. 8.
[2] L. Winstanley's *Introduction* to the *Faerie Queene*, Bk. I. p. lx.
[3] Percival's *Introduction* to Bk. I. p. lv.

for intellectual culture, speaks strongly of the necessity for the avoidance of sense-impression and this insistence on his part has been misunderstood by some as a defence of asceticism and regarded by them[1] as being opposed to the trend of Hellenic culture which has always preached the value of balance and harmony between the physical and mental powers of man. Nietzsche calls Plato 'a Christian before Christ' and there are frequent references elsewhere to the supposed vein of asceticism in him and to his exhortation to people to regard life as a preparation for death.[2] Plotinus has been open to the same interpretation as Plato, the more so as his personal life was extremely rigorous. But neither Plato nor Plotinus preached mortification of the flesh and torture of the body. Fasting, vigil and other austerities current in mediaeval times were not encouraged by either. As Dean Inge says, 'The ascetics of antiquity were not the Platonists but the Cynics whose object was to make themselves wholly independent of externals'.[3]

Plato has more than once emphasised the

---

[1] Dean Inge refers to Rohde and Nietzsche on the continent and to Livingstone in England.
[2] *Phaedo.*
[3] Inge's *Philosophy of Plotinus*, Vol. II. p. 166.

importance of gymnastics[1] and this proves his love of physical culture which can never be found in ascetics. The philosopher of Plato does not absolutely abhor physical comforts and things like 'costly raiments, or sandals, or other adornments of the body'. Socrates says, 'Instead of caring about them, does he not rather despise anything *more than nature needs?*'[2] Plotinus remarks, 'The good man will give to the body all that he sees to be useful and possible'. The pursuit of death which Plato describes as the object of the philosopher and the neglect of worldly pleasure preached by Plotinus, have no reference to the mortification of the flesh or the practice of austerities. What they mean is the gradual liberation of the human *mind* from *sense-impression,* the abandonment of sense-experience as a means of acquiring knowledge and the cultivation of what are called dianoetic virtues, pure and simple, based on the intuitions of the soul. Intellectual culture or *contemplation* is the object of both the philosophers, the reward for it being communion with Absolute Truth. The dominant note of Platonism and Neo-Platonism is intellectual, while that of Christianity is ethical, though the mediaeval

[1] *Republic*, II. 376.   [2] *Phaedo*, 64.

Christian Church highly valued physical purity. It is not asceticism or love of purity, moral and physical, that mainly characterises Plato and he cannot be called an ascetic and therefore un-Hellenic, as Livingstone would urge. On the contrary, the Hellenic love of knowledge finds fitting expression in Plato's conception of justice and in his hymn of dialectic; and in a study of the influence of Platonism and Neo-Platonism in Spenser, this intellectual aspect of their teachings should be clearly noted.

Undoubtedly, the mystical conception of Holiness based on Orphism in ancient Greece, which was marked by a sense of guilt requiring atonement, of pollution crying for purgation through ascetic discipline and mystical rites, e.g., sacramental meal regarded as an act of union with the divine, had its influence on Plato. But it is modified and rationalised in him.[1] Desire for union with the divine becomes *amor intellectualis* in Plato. The Orphic as well as the Platonic conception of Holiness was sadly wanting in the idea of love as a moral attribute. Moral likeness to God first enters into the conception of Holiness

---

[1] See the article on Holiness in the *Dictionary of Religion and Ethics*.

in Christianity and the operation of divine grace and mercy for the redemption of man is there based solely on the possibility of his realising the ideal of Holiness. Says Renwick, 'The Bible is the authority for Holiness as Aristotle is for Temperance and Justice'. It is this moral or Christian conception of Holiness as shaped by the idealism of the Protestant Church, and especially by the *Institutes* of Calvin, and not the Platonic Holiness or justice, that is allegorised by Spenser in Book I. of the *Faerie Queene*. According to Calvin, Holiness is the bond of union between man and God. He says,[1] 'It (i.e., the Scripture) has numerous admirable methods of recommending righteousness. . . With what better foundation can it begin than by reminding us that we must be *holy,* because God is *holy?*'[2] (Lev. 19 : 1 ; 1 Pet. 1 : 16). In Chapter VII. of Bk. III. of his *Institutes* Calvin insists on 'complete submission to the Holy Spirit' as a means of winning His grace, on charity, mercy and humility and in Chapter IX. on meditation on future life. The allegory in Bk. I. of the *Faerie Queene,* as Padelford points out, is one of 'the religious life of man (as painted

---

[1] *Institutes*, Bk. III. Ch. VI.
[2] See *Modern Philology*, Vol. XII. p. 10.

## 90    PLATONIC IDEAS IN SPENSER

by Calvin)—his conversion, training, and growth in grace'.[1]

In Plato the training in Holiness or justice, as depicted in Bk. VII. of the *Republic,* is purely intellectual. The holy man's progress lies through the mastery of sciences more and more abstract, until he is introduced to dialectic which enables him to commune with Truth. But the Redcrosse Knight's training, as symbolised in his adventures, is exclusively moral. His is a case of growth in humility and Christian moral virtues. To start with, he puts on the armour of St. Paul[2] before going out on his adventures. It consists of the sword of spirit, the helmet of salvation, the breastplate of righteousness, etc. He defeats Error and Atheism (Sansfoy), meets Spiritual Pride (Lucifera) and is betrayed by Falsehood (Duessa) into the clutches of Carnal Pride (Orgoglio). Rescued by Divine Grace (Arthur), he overcomes Despair and is purified and taught humility in the House of Holiness where he sees works of charity. The training in the virtue of Holiness as depicted here, is undoubtedly moral

---

[1] *Journal of English and Germanic Philology,* Vol. XXII. p. 3.
[2] See the Letter to Raleigh and Ephes. vi.

and Christian, and not intellectual or Platonic. Harrison, however, contends that the knight's ascent on the Hill of Contemplation and the view of Heavenly Jerusalem obtained by him signify intellectual training and its ultimate reward, viz., the vision of Truth as described in Plato. But a view of the Holy City from a mountain-top is a Biblical imagery which occurs in the Book of Revelation (Ch. XXI). The Hill of Contemplation may signify a state of mind which takes stock of its past worldly experiences and compares them with the glory of the celestial life promised to the virtuous man, as the hill in the Bible commands a view of the Holy City as well as of this world. It need not symbolise intellectual culture with its various stages of abstract knowledge as described in Bk. VII. of the *Republic*. It can also be interpreted to mean meditation on future life as explained by Calvin in Chapter IX. of Bk. III. of his *Institutes*. Calvinism requires active work of charity in young men and contemplation of the next world in the aged.[1] Redcrosse, therefore, is asked by the holy man to finish his adventure before settling on the Hill permanently.[2]

---

[1] *Institutes*, Bk. III. Ch. IX.
[2] *Faerie Queene*, Bk. I. C. x. st. 63.

Though the discipline undergone by Redcrosse is Christian and his progress is a growth in humility, grace and other moral attributes, the knight is accompanied in his journey by Una and her wisdom always protects him and gives him guidance. He is misled and entrapped inspite of his moral enthusiasm and inspite of the armour of St. Paul on his person just when Una is separated from him. The story of Bk. I. is not therefore an allegory of moral or religious life, pure and simple, but of moral life as strengthened by reason. The friendship between Guyon and Redcrosse seems to illustrate the same idea of reason going hand in hand with and sustaining moral or religious impulse. Though Holiness in Spenser is not of Aristotelian origin and his professed obligation to Aristotle cannot be literally true, it has been suggested by Jones that in making a synthesis of moral and intellectual or contemplative life, Spenser was influenced by the mediaeval Aristotelian tradition. 'However strictly we seek to interpret Spenser's declaration that his twelve private virtues are those that Aristotle has "devised", it is inconceivable that our poet in Christianising his Aristotle or in Aristotelianising his Christianity, should have been uninfluenced by the tradition of Christian Aristotelianism that carried over from the Middle Ages to the Renaissance'.[1] 'The approach to Christian ethics based upon Aristotle lies through the later peripatetic treatises entitled the *Eudemian Ethics* and the *Magna Moralia*'. There is a religious element in Aristotle's *Ethics* in addition to its rationalism. It says, e.g., 'He whose activity is directed by reason, and who . . . is in the best, i.e., the most rational state of mind, is also, as it seems, the most beloved of the Gods'.[2] 'It is clear that the gift of Nature is not in our own power, but is bestowed by some divine providence upon those who are truly fortunate'. Jones says, 'It is by developing the religious element already present in the *Nicomachean Ethics* and by giving ethical value to irrational impulse (i.e., of religion) that the peripatetic treatises (viz., the *Eudemian Ethics* and the *Magna Moralia*) approximate that view of the moral life, at once religious and rationalistic, which is so richly illustrated in the *Faerie Queene*'. The synthetic Christian ethics which, according to Jones, is at the background of the *Faerie Queene,* received large contributions from Thomas Aquinas and Melanchthon, the chief expositors of

---

[1] *Journal of English and Germanic Philology*, Vol. XXV. p. 284.
[2] *Ethics*, Bk. X. Ch. X.

morality for Catholic and Protestant Europe respectively. With some modifications, the correlation of contemplative life to the life of action noticeable in the *Ethics* (Bk. I. ch. XIII) is reproduced in both these teachers. Both lay down that the life of contemplation is the highest good of man and produces the greatest happiness, but unlike Plato whose transcendental rationalism led to a rift in his philosophy which was later responsible for the exaltation of monastic life in the Middle Ages, they relate it to practical (or religious) life as the stepping-stone to it. Jones points out the possible influence of the ethical systems of these two teachers on Spenser's *Faerie Queene* and thinks that their synthesis of religious and contemplative life finds recognition in the allegories of the House of Holiness and the Hill of Contemplation. 'The Catholic ethic here (i.e. in Bk. I.) abundantly illustrated is in full harmony with the Catholic spiritual *discipline* of the House of Holiness. But there, carried beyond the cardinal and infused virtues, the system of Catholic ethics is made complete by giving us a glimpse of that life of contemplation in which there will be full exercise for the *intellectual* virtues of Sapientia, Scientia and Intellectus, which lead the aspiring soul beyond the sphere of human responsibilities and human perplexities to ecstatic union with the divine'.[1]  Jones continues, 'Like Thomas Aquinas, Melanchthon notes as the highest activity that of *knowing* God and *obeying* him . . . "If Aristotle", says Melanchthon, "had considered the fundamental distinctions among actions, he would have placed *virtue* in relation to this *knowledge* of God. But . . . one can always attach himself to the Aristotelian view if one only remembers that *knowing* God is the highest *virtue* and that all virtues are to be related to God"'. Though he makes no reference to the mediaeval Aristotelian tradition, Kitchin speaks of the blending of reason and morality as the theme of Bk. I. 'In the first Book the Christian comes out firmly assured in his belief, and that, not as a mere effort of the imagination, or as a devotional sentiment, but as a severe intellectual inquiry and sifting of the truth, a "proving all things" in order to "hold fast that which is good". For this combination of reason with religion was deemed not only allowable but essential in the 16th century, and bore fruit in the appeals to men's judgment and personal reason as against authority, to common sense as against

[1] *Journal of English and Germanic Philology*, Vol. XXV. p. 291.

## 96  PLATONIC IDEAS IN SPENSER

the iron rules and quibbles of the later scholastics, to the personal study of the Bible as against a blind reliance on a traditional and sacerdotal system'.[1]

Book I. closes with the marriage of Redcrosse and Una—Holiness and Truth. Though the discipline undergone by the knight, the seeker for Truth, is traceable to Christian ethics as shaped by the mediaeval Aristotelian tradition and Calvinism, the ideal of Truth is borrowed from Plato. Spenser is responsible for many incongruous combinations of imageries and thoughts and the combination of Christian discipline with Platonic idealism may be mentioned as one of them. That Una represents Truth, the object of pure intellectual activity, is explicitly stated[2] by Spenser himself more than once. With Una at his side, Redcrosse easily defeats the monster Error. Her wisdom is seen in the skill with which she guides Redcrosse during his journey. She is thus different from Duessa (or Falsehood) who leads him into the House of Pride and then into the clutches of Orgoglio. Danger always finds Una at his side planning his rescue and when the knight is defeated and imprisoned by Orgoglio,

[1] *Introduction* to the *Faerie Queene*, Bk. II. p. v.
[2] See the arguments to Cantos II. and III. of Bk. I.

## TRUTH

Una effects his rescue with the help of Arthur. In describing his perils, Spenser notes how

'—stedfast *truth* acquite him out of all'.
(Bk. I. C. VIII. st. 1.)

Again, when Redcrosse is bent on killing himself at the instigation of Despair, it is Una's argument that convinces him of his error of judgment. Here also Una breathes the very spirit of wisdom. Redcrosse falls in danger and the snares of Duessa entrap him only when he is deprived of the guidance of Una or Truth. In Canto VI. her wisdom brings the satyrs and the fauns of the forest under her subjection and

'— her gentle *wit* she plyes
To teach them *truth*,'—(C. VI. st. 19.)

Spirit of wisdom as she is, her gift to them is Truth.

Truth is marked by permanence, stability and unity. These are also the characteristics of the beauty of Una which has always the same quiet effulgence. Her love of Redcrosse and her very name[1] signify her inner nature and her character— her unchangeableness and simplicity. Plotinus

---
[1] Una means *one*; Grosart, however, derives Una from the Irish Oonagh, a fairy queen.

calls the ultimate Reality the One. The evanescence of sensible objects is indicated by their rapid changes of form, and hence Duessa[1] too often changes her lover and too frequently changes her appearance. Her ravishing beauty vanishes and she turns out to be an ugly hag when she is detected and punished by Arthur. That Spenser personifies Platonic Truth in Una, is further evident from his conception of her beauty. In Plato Truth is wonderfully beautiful.[2] Earthly beauty is a mere copy of its celestial beauty which can be perceived not by the eye but only by the mind after it has been purged of the grossness of sense-impression. 'Sight is the keenest of our bodily senses; though not by that is wisdom seen'. Hence, though Una is supremely beautiful, Spenser never describes her beauty as an object of visual perception. In fact, there is a veil covering her face which lies altogether hidden from Redcrosse's sight. The wonderful nature of her beauty is only indirectly suggested by the poet's reference to the admiration[3] felt by the sylvan creatures for her lovely face when her veil is snatched away by Sansloy. Drawn to her presence by her cry for help,

[1] She is copied from Ariosto's Alcina.
[2] See *Phaedrus*, 250.    [3] C. VI. st. 12.

## TRUTH

'All stand astonied at her beautie bright'—
(C. VI. st. 9.)

Sylvanus himself had never seen such loveliness and the nymphs of the forest are ashamed of their own much-vaunted beauty when they see Una.[1] It is to be noticed that Spenser does not use a single word to indicate the nature of the physical charms of Una; yet he can, if necessary, give the most detailed description of woman's beauty. He describes Britomart in Bk. IV. and his own beloved in the *Epithalamion* in this manner. But the beauty of Truth is Beauty Absolute, and to use ordinary language and ordinary imagery with reference to it, can only have the effect of circumscribing and misinterpreting it.

The final meeting between Redcrosse and Una in Canto XII., after the knight's purification in the House of Holiness and the killing of the dragon (Sin), also suggests the influence of Plato. Though in Plato Truth is not an object of visual perception, its apprehension by the purified mind is figured forth as a glorious vision in the *Symposium*[2] and in the *Phaedrus*.[3] Beauty is a mark of Truth and hence, when the knight triumphs over impurity (the dragon), the veil of Una is removed

[1] C. VI. st. 18.   [2] *Symposium*, 211.
[3] *Phaedrus*, 247.

and the transcendent beauty of Truth flashes on the eyes of Redcrosse. Prior to this (in Canto X.), the knight had gained the reward of his training in Christian discipline in the House of Holiness in having a vision of Heavenly Jerusalem. It has been pointed out that this latter means the same thing in Christian Theology as the ideal of Truth does in Greek Philosophy and, as a matter of fact, the Greek idea gradually changed into this Christian form with the growth of Christianity.[1] The fact that Spenser supplements the knight's reward in the Christian form by another in the Platonic form, viz., by a vision of Una's beauty, also shows the influence of Plato. Again, beauty in the *Symposium* is the object of love and hence love becomes the ultimate link between Redcrosse and Una.

—' her owne *deare loved* knight,
All were she daily with himselfe in place,
Did *wonder* much at her celestiall sight ' :
(C. XII. st. 23).

The marriage of Una and Redcrosse as painted by Spenser indicates further the influence of Neo-Platonic mysticism on the poet. Mystics recognise a form of communion more direct and more inti-

[1] See the article on Christianity in the *Encyclopaedia Britannica*.

mate than intellection. Though it is usually figured forth as a vision, it really baffles analysis and description. It is a matter of inner realisation and is therefore called a union—union of the seeker with the object of his search. This, however, is a turn of thought which is not to be met with in Plato. His vision may be something more direct than mere intellectual comprehension, but it is less than union. 'Plato nowhere gives a hint of *that mystical vision* wherein the seer and the seen *merge together* in one indistinguishable act of objectless contemplation'.[1] Plotinus, however, in one of his *Enneads* attempts to explain this mystic union between the perceiver and the perceived.[2] Spenser has allegorised in Bk. I. this aspect of Neo-Platonic mysticism. The beauty of Una is indeed at first revealed to Redcrosse as a glorious vision as in the *Phaedrus* of Plato, but the Neo-Platonic idea of the merging of the beholder in the beheld or the union of the two, is figured later on in the marriage of Una and Redcrosse—in the holy *union* of wedlock as it is generally called.

Thus there seems to be present in Bk. I. not merely the influence of Plato, as Miss Winstanley

[1] P. E. More's *Hellenistic Philosophies*, p. 184.
[2] See *post* Chapter VII.

and Harrison[1] have suggested, but also of the mysticism of Plotinus. Renwick[2] clearly notes this when he refers to the 'slightest mystical infusion in the last canto' of Book I.

Miss Winstanley suggests[3] that there is a parallelism between the story of Redcrosse and Una and that of Arthur's quest for Gloriana who, she thinks, is meant as a 'type of the Heavenly Wisdom which, as Plato says, is the most resplendent and glorious of all the ideas'. Whatever might have been the intention of Spenser, no Platonic touch appears in Gloriana as it does in Una. In fact, Gloriana remains a vague ideal in the background and Spenser never attempts to give any estimate of her nature and personality. There is no special point in suggesting Plato's influence in the conception of her character, unless Miss Winstanley means by Platonic influence idealism generally. Idealism has a close affinity with the Platonic form of thought and it easily lends itself to expression through Platonic imagery. The *Faerie Queene* has been called 'one long idealising' and even if those of its features

---

[1] See *Platonism in English Poetry*, p. 1.
[2] *Edmund Spenser*, p. 161.
[3] *Introduction* to the *Faerie Queene*, Bk. I. p. lxv.

# TRUTH

which have been pointed out as the mark of Plato's influence be otherwise explained away—if, for example, Una be regarded exclusively as Gospel Truth,—the general outlook of the poem and its spirit of idealism may still be regarded as the outcome of the impress of Platonic philosophy on Spenser. As Padelford says[1], '. . . . if the spirit of the allegory is primarily Christian, we must not overlook the fact that its mystic idealism is akin to that of Plato, and that the moral courage of its hero and the conception of life as moral warfare are Platonic as well as Christian'.

Miss Winstanley says that Arthur's shield typifies Platonic Truth. It is made of diamond[2] and is unfading, its brilliance surpasses even that of the sun[3] and only the pure can gaze upon it, for it turns others blind.[4] Here indeed is noticeable some closeness of the parallel to Plato's account of Truth; but this description of the shield, if it be symbolical, equally applies to the Christian idea of faith. The shield of faith recommended by St. Paul for a Christian[5] is borne by Redcrosse.

---

[1] *Journal of English and Germanic Philology*, Vol. XXII. p. 4.
[2] C. VII. st. 33.   [3] C. VII. st. 34.
[4] *Ibid.* st. 35.   [5] Ephes. vi.

Arthur represents in Bk. I. the same virtue as Redcrosse and Arthur's shield is very likely the same in quality as Redcrosse's. Moreover, the enemy overcome with the shield is Orgoglio[1] or carnal pride which is the eternal antagonist of faith. In a recent article on this topic Pienaar also explains Arthur's shield as faith and rejects another view that it represents the Bible.

There are some minor matters not connected with the main allegory in Bk. I., where Spenser has borrowed from Plato. The wood of Error represents the entanglements of matter and opinion enwrapping man's soul in this world, the false image of Una means the deceipt of untruth[2] and the reply of Redcrosse to the arguments of Despair advising suicide, is borrowed from the well-known speech of Socrates in the *Phaedo*.

The allegory of Holiness in the *Faerie Queene* had many literary forerunners. Stephen Hawes' *Pastime of Pleasure* invites comparison with it as being its model in many respects. Mrs. Browning says that it is one of 'the four columnar marbles on whose foundation is exalted into light the great allegorical poem of the world, Spenser's

---

[1] Bk. I. C. VIII.  [2] See *Phaedo*, 79.

*Faerie Queene'*. George Saintsbury, on the other hand, thinks that Hawes' work had very little influence on Spenser's poem. Whatever might be the nature and extent of Spenser's obligation to Hawes in respect of his allegorical method, the difference in tone and outlook between their two poems, due to Spenser's Platonic idealism, is very clear. In form, the *Pastime of Pleasure* bears a close resemblance to the Legend of Holiness, both being narratives of chivalric adventure. In each the hero is rewarded with the hand of a lady on the completion of his adventure. St. Paul's armour, the house of purification, the tale-bearer, giants as types of moral evil and the dragon figure prominently in both the poems. But even when allowances have been made for the immature literary workmanship of Hawes, there remains a world of difference between Redcrosse and Una on the one hand and Graund Amour and Pucell on the other. The idealism of Plato also makes itself felt in Spenser in the reward which comes to Redcrosse. Una is a sublime conception,—she is almost an abstraction. As the symbol of Abstract Truth, she remains veiled throughout her journey. But Hawes' heroine La Bell Pucell is too much of a creature of the flesh. While the union of Una and Redcrosse is described by Spenser as a glorious vision and an indissoluble tie in delicate language, Hawes is frankly realistic in referring to the blandishments showered by Graund Amour on La Bell Pucell.

# CHAPTER IV

## FRIENDSHIP

FRIENDSHIP in Spenser's *Faerie Queene,* Bk. IV. has no well-defined meaning, but conveys different ideas at different places. Warren says, 'Friendliness, unanimity, good-will, friendship and love in the spiritual sense—are all mingled in Spenser's term Friendship'.[1] The sources of his idea of Friendship, too, are more than one, though Aristotle is drawn upon more largely than Plato.

The origin of the Hellenic conception of Friendship has already been discussed.[2] The *Lysis,* Plato's dialogue on Friendship,[3] contains, in a way, a repetition of the arguments of Diotima in the *Symposium.* The theme in the *Symposium* is love and her efforts are seriously directed to a satisfactory solution of the problem with the assistance of imagination. In the *Lysis* the subject-matter of enquiry is similar to that in the *Symposium* and it is called Friendship; but the way in which

---
[1] *Introduction* to the *Faerie Queene,* Bk. IV.
[2] See *ante* Chapter II.
[3] A profound conception of friendship is also to be met with outside Greek philosophy, e.g., in the literature of the Hindus as also in that of the Sufis of Persia.

Socrates exposes the contradictions that arise in course of the discussion, shows his genuine desire of finding out the truth with the help of reason. The conclusion at which Socrates seems to arrive in the *Lysis,* after rejecting a number of plausible theories, is that those who are neither good nor bad are the friends of the good, because the good are as incapable of friendship amongst themselves as the bad. This is similar to Diotima's conclusion (in respect of love) in the *Symposium.* But apart from the conclusions, throughout the numerous arguments and the shifting grounds in the speeches in the *Symposium* and the *Lysis,* there runs the idea of the universal association of the good with love and Friendship. Whether love and friendship are logically possible between good and good or between good and that which is neither good nor bad ('congenial'), the idea of the good is always present in Plato's thoughts on these topics. And this is what struck Aristotle who, as a practical moralist, was probably unwilling to follow Plato's abstruse arguments and subtle distinctions and who failed to see why, in Plato's opinion, friendship between good people was not possible. In classifying Friendship, he assigned the very first place to it. In the *Faerie Queene* it is the Aristotelian idea

# FRIENDSHIP

of Friendship or love of the good for each other that is to be met with, though it had been rejected by Plato as illogical. Aristotle thus defines perfect Friendship without however assigning any reasons for his view: 'The perfect friendship or love is the friendship or love of people who are good and alike in virtue, for these people are alike in wishing each other's good, in so far as they are good, and they are good in themselves. . . . Their friendship therefore continues as long as their virtue, and virtue is a permanent quality'.[1] This is based on the following idea of Friendship which Plato had laid aside as untenable: 'The good are like one another and friends to one another'.[2]

Spenser's portrayal of Cambell and Triamond shows traces of this conception of Friendship. Their friendship is called a tie of virtue in so many words and Spenser thinks that

'— *vertue is the band* that bindeth harts most sure'.[3]
(Bk. IV. C. II. st. 29.)

Plato does not believe in wicked people's capacity for friendship. According to him, they

---

[1] *Ethics*, Bk. VIII. ch. IV.  [2] *Lysis*, 214.
[3] See also C. IX. st. 1.

are 'passionate and restless, and anything which is at variance and enmity with itself is not likely to be in union or harmony with any other thing'.[1] Aristotle thinks that such people have not even that steady and consistent self-love the extension of which leads to friendship. 'Such people are at variance with themselves, and while desiring one set of things, wish for something else. They are, e.g., incontinent people; they choose not what seems to themselves good, but what is pleasant, although it is injurious'.[2] Following these two philosophers, Spenser says,

' — in *base mind* nor friendship dwels nor enmity.'
(C. IV. st. 11.)

Though Aristotle is at one with Plato in believing that no true friendship can possibly exist between persons who are unable to perceive the beauty of noble character and virtue, yet, as a practical man, he has not ignored combinations which wicked people often form amongst themselves for seeking profit or pleasure. He has put such combinations in the second class of friendship (the first class having been reserved for what he calls perfect friendship between virtuous people). Such combinations are shortlived. In Spenser a combina-

[1] *Lysis*, 214.   [2] *Ethics*, Bk. VIII.

## FRIENDSHIP

tion of this kind exists between Blandamour and Paridell whose alliance depends on their expectation of profit. There are also some details where Spenser follows Aristotle.

In the opening stanzas to Book IV. of the *Faerie Queene* is found another conception of friendship which is solely derived from Plato and to which there is no parallel in Aristotle. Spenser uses the word 'love', and not 'friendship' in these stanzas and in reality they sing of noble love as discussed in the speech of Phaedrus in the *Symposium*. Spenser celebrates one aspect of this love as chastity in Book III. of the *Faerie Queene*.[1] In the introductory stanzas to Book IV., Friendship or this love is the bond of union between human beings irrespective of sex exactly as in the speech of Phaedrus, while in Book III. it means the most sacred relationship between man and woman. Love in Bk. IV.

'— of honor and all vertue is
The roote, and brings forth glorious flowres of fame,
That crowne true lovers with immortall blis',—
(Bk. IV. Introductory Stanza 2.)

Spenser gives a different meaning to Friendship in Canto X. of Book IV. The character of

[1] See *ante* Chapter II.

## 112  PLATONIC IDEAS IN SPENSER

Concord typifies this meaning and Discord in Canto I. only spoils[1] the work accomplished by Concord who represents cosmogonic love. Concord is described as the mother of Peace and Friendship and is an 'amiable Dame'. The creation of the world is the result of her benign influence and of the feeling of love or Friendship implanted by her in the elements which were previously in a state of perpetual warfare known as chaos. Concord is thus described:

> ' By her the heaven is in his course contained,
> And all the world in state unmoved stands,
> As their Almightie maker first ordained,
> And bound them with inviolable bands;
> Else would the waters overflow the lands,
> And fire devoure the ayre, and hell them quight,
> But that she holds them with her blessed hands.'
> (C. X. st. 35.)

Discord in Canto I. is just the opposite of Concord as described above.[2]

The description of the harmony into which the primeval elements settled down at the creation of the world as love or Friendship is very old in Greek philosophy. In the *Symposium* Eryximachus deals with the harmonious blending of

[1] C. I. st. 29.      [2] C. I. st. 30.

different humours in man's constitution, in the course of the seasons, etc., in order to show that the same principle of order and balance manifests itself in the human body as well as in inanimate objects. Everywhere the blending of different elements leads to disorder or evil, if it violates proportion; this is vulgar love as opposed to perfect love. 'The best Physician is one who is able to separate fair love from foul, or to convert one into the other and if he is a skilful practitioner, he knows how to eradicate and how to implant love whichever is required; and he can reconcile the most hostile elements in the constitution and make them friends. Now the most hostile are the most opposite, such as hot and cold, moist and dry, bitter and sweet, and the like. And my ancestor, Asclepius, knowing how to implant friendship and accord in these elements was the creator of our art . . . The course of the seasons is also full of both principles, and when, as I was saying, the elements of hot and cold, moist and dry, attain the harmonious love of one another and blend in temperance and harmony, they bring to men, animals and vegetables, health and wealth, and do them no harm, whereas the wantonness and overbearingness of the other love affecting the seasons is a great

## 114  PLATONIC IDEAS IN SPENSER

injurer and destroyer, and is the source of Pestilence . . . .'[1] Ficinus applies this idea of a harmonious blending of different elements in the human body and in the course of the seasons to the creation[2] of the world. Spenser personifies the urge for creative union inherent in the elements as Concord and their tendency to disorder as Discord in Book IV. The conception of cosmogonic love re-appears in the *Hymne in Honour of Love* and *Colin Clout*.[3]

---

[1] Speech of Eryximachus.

[2] Renwick who stresses the influence of Lucretius on Spenser, especially refers to Spenser's description of the Court of Venus in support of his contention. Though he admits the influence of Aristotle's *Ethics*, e.g., of his idea of *Philia* on Bk. IV. of the *Faerie Queene*, Renwick points out that this description contains the first thirty-odd lines of Lucretius' *de Rerum Natura*. (See *Edmund Spenser*, p. 154.)

[3] See *post* Chapter V.

# NEO-PLATONISM

## CHAPTER V

### THEORIES OF BEAUTY AND LOVE—INFLUENCE OF ITALIAN NEO-PLATONISTS

PLATO is specially noted as the propounder of theories of beauty and love; but it is these theories that have been most copiously elaborated by Italian Neo-Platonists who have not touched other Platonic doctrines, e.g., the theory of harmony in the soul. Amplifications by different Italian writers have proceeded almost along the same lines and it is difficult to distinguish their views. There is a striking resemblance between Spenser's ideas of beauty and love and theirs and only this can be pointed out to indicate the English poet's obligation to Italian Neo-Platonism in general. It is not possible to go beyond this always and to trace definitely the influence of any individual author—Bembo, Romei, Pico or Castiglione—on Spenser's work, though clear traces of Ficinus' interpretation of Plato and Plotinus are discernible in Spenser as much as in almost all the later Italian Neo-Platonists.

Spenser in his *Hymne in Honour of Beautie*

proceeds first to account for the beauty of the external world and next to explain human beauty. His theory that material things are beautiful, because they have been created by God[1] according to the Pattern of perfect Beauty which pours its influence on them and irradiates them, is a blend of Plato and Plotinus. Its first part, viz., that the world has been modelled by God on a beautiful Pattern is borrowed from Plato.[2] Spenser identifies the Pattern of the *Timaeus* with Abstract or Perfect Beauty which in the *Symposium* is the last of a long series of beautiful objects. He says:

' That wondrous Paterne, wheresoere it bee,
. . . , . . . . . .
Is perfect Beautie, which all men adore;—'

The Pattern of the *Timaeus* appears in many later writers. Romei calls it proportion but makes it reside in divine intellect. He says, 'Proportion which, in God, is part of His beauty, is nothing but idea and the ideal form of the universe existing in the divine intellect, as the model and ideal form of an edifice exists in the soul of the architect with greater beauty than is to be discovered in the edifice itself'.[3]

[1] *Hymne in Honour of Beautie*, st. 5–7.
[2] See the *Timaeus*, 28.
[3] Romei's *Discorsi*, Giornata Prima.

As regards the manner, described in the second part of Spenser's theory, in which beauty is imparted to material objects, both the *Symposium* and the *Phaedo* state that it is unknown. Socrates says, for example, 'I . . . am assured in my own mind that nothing makes a thing beautiful but the presence and participation of beauty in whatever way or manner obtained; for as to the manner, I am uncertain but I stoutly contend that by beauty all beautiful things become beautiful'.[1] The *Timaeus* suggests that the beauty of the world (as of all living creatures) is due to something which is not material and which has been put into it by God. The *Phaedrus* gives a definite idea of the process of derivation of beauty by material objects, which is called *effluence*. Referring to the change which comes upon the lover's soul when it beholds the beauty of the beloved, Plato says, 'As he (lover) receives the *effluence of beauty* through the eyes, the wing moistens and he warms. As he warms, the parts out of which the wing grew, and which had been hitherto closed and rigid, and had prevented the wing from shooting forth, are melted, and as nourishment streams upon him, the lower end of the wing begins to swell and grow

[1] *Phaedo*, 100.

from the root upwards; and the growth extends under the whole soul'.[1] The stream of beauty passing through the lover's eyes and helping the growth of the wings of his soul, is again mentioned by Plato in referring to the story of Zeus and Ganymede. The growth of the wings signifies the infusion of beauty into the soul, preparing it for its higher flights.

This idea in the *Phaedrus* is fully developed by Plotinus in *An Essay on the Beautiful* which propounds a theory of aesthetics absent from Plato. Matter, according to this Neo-Platonist, is formless, incorporeal and chaotic. Reason cannot comprehend it except as indefiniteness. It can have no magnitude or bulk. 'It is, however, a void bulk . . . The indefiniteness of it, likewise, is a bulk of this kind'. Into this 'void bulk' which, according to ordinary imagery, would be the crevices or fissures in a solid object, the so-called rays of beauty fit themselves, and these then irradiate, beautify or rationalise matter by combining its parts into a complete whole. 'It is by participation of species that we call every sensible object beautiful . . . Whatever is entirely remote from this immortal source is perfectly base and deformed. And such is matter, which by its

[1] *Phaedrus*, 251.

## THEORIES OF BEAUTY AND LOVE 119

nature is ever averse from the *supervening irradiations of form*. Whenever, therefore, form accedes, it conciliates in amicable unity the parts which are about to compose a whole; for being itself one, it is not wonderful that the subject of its power *should tend to unity,* as far as the nature of a compound will admit. Hence beauty is established in multitude when the many is reduced into one'.[1] Plotinus describes Absolute Beauty as the sun and its influence as the rays of the sun, the operation of the two being taken to be analogous. Ficinus says, 'Beauty is splendour. It penetrates all things'.[2] Echoes of this are also to be found in other Italian Neo-Platonists. Says Bembo, for example, 'Just as stars take their light from the sun, so all these beautiful things take their quality from the divine and eternal beauty.'[3]
'. . . parlando della bellezza che noi intendemo', Castiglione says, '. . diremo, che è un flusso della bontà divina, il quale si spanda sopra tutte le cose create, come il lume del sole'.[4] Romei says, 'Beauty is born of *form* and therefore all things that are beautiful, are said to have form. Ugliness

[1] Plotinus' *An Essay on the Beautiful*, tr. T. Taylor.
[2] See L. Winstanley's *Introduction* to the *Fowre Hymnes*, p. lxii.
[3] *Degli Asolani*, Libro III.
[4] *Il Cortegiano*, Libro Quarto, LII.

is born of matter which, inasmuch as it is without form by its own nature, is the source of all deformity'.[1] Spenser adopts this theory and, referring to the Pattern, he says,

> 'Thereof as every earthly thing partakes
> Or more or lesse, by influence divine,
> So it more faire accordingly it makes,—
> . .    . .    . .    . .    . .
> For, through infusion of celestiall powre,
> The duller earth it quickneth with delight,
> And life-full spirits privily doth powre
> Through all the parts, that to the lookers sight
> They seeme to please;'[2]

The figure used by Plotinus to explain the effluence of beauty into matter is also retained by Spenser. In one poem he speaks of the Pattern as the 'lampe' or as the 'starre' and its influence as the 'beame'.[3]

In treating human beauty, Spenser follows closely Italian Neo-Platonists like Ficinus, Castiglione and Pico. At the very outset, he mocks at the popular idea of beauty, viz., that it is the effect of colour and symmetry of form. He writes:

> 'How vainely then doe ydle wits invent,
>     That beautie is nought else but mixture made

---

[1] *Discorsi*, Giornata Prima.
[2] *Hymne in Honour of Beautie*, st. 7–8.
[3] *Ibid.* st. 7, 8, 16.

## THEORIES OF BEAUTY AND LOVE

    Of colours faire, and goodly temp'rament
    Of pure complexions,—
    . .    . .    . .    . .    . .
    Or that it is but comely composition
    Of parts well measurd, with meet disposition!' [1]

These lines are taken almost *verbatim* from Plotinus. He says, 'It is the general opinion that a certain commensuration of parts to each other, and to the whole, with the addition of colour, generates that beauty which is the object of sight; and that in the commensurate and the moderate alone the beauty of everything consists'.[2] Pico is equally emphatic in his opposition to the popular notion of beauty which he discusses in the manner of Plotinus and Ficinus, only to point out its untenable character. He writes: 'Corporeal beauty implies, first the material disposition of the Body, consisting of quantity in the proportion and distance of parts, of quality in figure and colour: secondly, a certain quality which cannot be exprest by any term better than Gracefulness, shining in all that is fair. This is properly Venus, Beauty, which kindles the fire of Love in Mankinde: they who affirm it results from the disposition of the Body, the sight, figure, and colour of features, are easily confuted by experience.

[1] *H. B.* st. 10.      [2] *An Essay on the Beautiful.*

We see many persons exact, and unaccusable in every part, destitute of this grace, and comelinesse ; others lesse perfect in those particular conditions, excellently graceful and comely'.[1] Romei expresses the same idea in almost the same language : 'Without grace, beauty is not pleasing and would not be pleasing, because accompanied by grace, she, i.e., beauty has the power to capture all those souls that can know her. Without grace, beauty may be said to be imperfect, and hence the ancients made the Graces the maids of Venus'.[2]

According to the Neo-Platonists, the irresistible conclusion is that human beauty or grace must be connected with the soul. The passion of love can only be explained on the theory that beauty which generates it in the lover's mind, is not a foreign element but something akin to the mind or the soul to which its appeal lies. The apparently sensuous beauty of the human figure is but the manifestation of the beautiful soul within. Ficinus says, 'Since matters are thus related, it must necessarily be that beauty is a something common to virtue, figure and voices (i.e., not an attribute of the body only). From which it is apparent that

[1] Pico's *Discourse*, commentary on st. 6-8.
[2] *Discorsi*, Giornata Prima.

## THEORIES OF BEAUTY AND LOVE

the essence of beauty cannot be bodies (or matter); because if beauty were material, it would not agree with the virtues of the soul which are immaterial'.[1]

A soul is beautiful or ugly in proportion as it is emancipated from the thraldom of sense and approaches the plane of Intellect or Divinity. Says Plotinus, 'The soul, thus defined (i.e., as ornamented with such virtues as temperance, fortitude, magnanimity, etc.), becomes form and reason, is altogether incorporeal and *intellectual,* and wholly participates of that divine nature which is the fountain of loveliness. Hence the soul *reduced to intellect becomes astonishingly beautiful.*' It is such a rationalised soul that beautifies the body. About the formative energy of the beautiful or intelligent soul Plotinus remarks, 'Bodies themselves participate of beauty from the soul which, as something *divine,* and a portion of the beautiful itself, renders whatever it supervenes and subdues, beautiful as far as its natural capacity will admit'. The relation between the soul and the Intellect or Divinity and the formative power of the human soul are also referred to by Romei and Castiglione. 'I say that as the beauty of the

[1] Translated from Ficinus' *Commentarium in Convivium,* V. The Latin passage is reproduced by L. Winstanley in her *Introduction* to the *Fowre Hymnes,* p. lxii.

## 124 PLATONIC IDEAS IN SPENSER

human body is chiefly placed in the upper part which sees the heavenly light, so the beauty of the human soul is in the most eminent part of the soul which is exposed to the divine light : this is called Intellect'.[1] 'Man, filled with wonder by looking at human beauty, may raise his mind to the contemplation of the *true and essential beauty* of which this (beauty) is the shadow and image'.[2] Castiglione says, 'Della bellezza de' quali (corpi) la piú propinqua causa estimo io che sia la bellezza dell'anima, che, come partecipe di quella vera bellezza divina, illustra e fa bello ciò ch' ella tocca, .... però la bellezza è il vero trofeo della vittoria dell'anima, quando essa con la virtú divina signoreggia la natura materiale, e col suo lume vince le tenebre del corpo.'[3] Again, 'Parlando della bellezza che noi intendemo, che è quella solamente che appar nei corpi e massimamente nei volti umani . . . diremo, che è un flusso della bontà divina, il quale .... quando trova un volto ben misurato e composto con una certa gioconda concordia di colori distinti, ed aiutati dai lumi e dall'ombre e da una ordinata distanzia e termini di linee, vi s'infonde e si

---
[1] Romei's *Discorsi*, Giornata Prima.
[2] *Discorsi*.
[3] *Il Cortegiano*, Libro Quarto, LIX.

## THEORIES OF BEAUTY AND LOVE 125

dimostra bellissimo'.[1] Ficinus describes 'the descent of the soul from heaven to form the body, and the correspondence between the beautiful soul and the beautiful body ; the reason why a beautiful soul sometimes forms only an ugly body'.[2] He thus explains his idea : 'Whatever soul is born upon earth under the ascendency of Jove, makes for itself a body in which the influence of Jove predominates. The model is first made in ether and afterwards carried out in material form. If the soul finds suitable matter, it can mould it exactly to the type, but if the matter is unsuitable, it is not able to do this.'[3]

The ideas of Plotinus and Ficinus are elaborated by Pico according to whom God scatters souls on the planets—'some in the Moon, others in other planets and stars'. The nature of a soul varies according to the planet on which it is cast. 'Platonists affirm some souls are of the nature of Saturn, others of Jupiter or some other planet ; meaning, one soul hath more conformity in its Nature with the soul of the Heaven of Saturn than

---

[1] *Il Cortegiano.*
[2] *Cambridge History of English Literature*, Vol. III. p. 217.
[3] *Commentarium in Convivium*, VI. 6 translated at p. lxvi. of L. Winstanley's *Introduction* to the *Fowre Hymnes.*

with that of Jupiter'. 'Many imagine the Rational Soul descending from her star, in her "Vehiculum Coeleste", of her self forms the Body, to which by that medium she is united . . . Into the "Vehiculum" of the Soul, by her endued with Power to form the Body, is infused from her star a particular formative vertue, distinct according to that star; thus the aspect of one is Saturnine, of another jovial, etc. In their looks we reade the nature of their souls."[1] Of human beauty Pico says, 'This then must by consequence be ascribed to the Soul; which, when perfect and lucid, transfuseth even into the Body some beams of its splendour'. All these notions about the derivation of the soul from God ('immortall *spright*' in st. 16, *H.B.*), its planetary home (*H.B.* st. 15), its descent into human body (*H.B.* st. 17) and the irradiation of dull matter by it, find a place in Spenser's poetry. About the soul the poet says:—

> ' When she in fleshly seede is eft enraced,
> Through every *part she doth the same impresse*,'—[2]
> . . . . . . . . . .
> ' Therof it comes that these faire soules, which have
> The most resemblance of that heavenly light,

[1] Pico's *Discourse*, commentary on st. 6–8
[2] *H. B.* st. 17.

## THEORIES OF BEAUTY AND LOVE

Frame to themselves most beautifull and brave
Their fleshly bowre, most fit for their delight,
And the grosse matter by a soveraine might
Tempers so trim, that it may well be seene
A pallace fit for such a virgin Queene '.[1]

From the proposition that the formative energy of the soul shapes for it a body commensurate with its beauty, the Neo-Platonists have easily arrived at its converse, viz., that a beautiful person has always a virtuous soul and beauty is the index of noble ancestry. Castiglione holds similar views about the connection between physical beauty and moral worth.[2] He concludes: 'I brutti adunque per lo piú sono ancor mali, e li belli boni'.[3] Spenser says,—

' — where-ever that thou doest behold
A comely corpse, with beautie faire endewed,
Know this for certaine, that the same doth hold
A beauteous soule, with faire conditions thewed '—
                                    (*H. B.* st. 20.)

To those who protest against such a sweeping generalisation and point the finger at handsome men given to vice, the Neo-Platonists' reply is

[1] *H. B.* st. 18.
The sun was regarded as a planet in the Ptolemaic system of astronomy. Spenser describes the sun as the ' native planet ' of the soul which comes down to it from God and derives from it its peculiar virtues.
[2] *Il Cortegiano*, Libro Quarto, LVII.
[3] *Ibid*. LVIII.

## 128  PLATONIC IDEAS IN SPENSER

that matter is not always amenable to the discipline of the soul. According to Ficinus, the beautiful soul 'keeps constantly ready to inform and adorn with wonderful effect the shapelessness of matter. If anything hideous, therefore, occurs in Nature, it occurs against that first intention of God and of Nature, just as when anything distorted is produced in an artist's studio, it is produced against the artist's intention'.[1] This idea is also traceable in Ficinus' follower Pico and in Benivieni whose *Ode of Love* was the subject-matter of Pico's *Discourse*. The rebellion of matter against the formative activity of the soul is suggested in the following lines of Benivieni :—

> '. . . . now as she may
> With instruments like hers, in human clay
> She frames her house; and that must mould and form
> Which thwarts now more, now less, her high designs'.
>
> (*Ode of Love*, St. 6.)

Pico's comment on these lines runs thus : 'In their (i.e., men's) looks we reade the nature of their souls. But because inferiour matter is not ever obedient to the Stamp, the vertue of the Soul

---

[1] *Plotini Divini illius è Platonica familia Philosophi De rebus Philosophicis*, Lib. LIII. Basilea. MDLIX.

## THEORIES OF BEAUTY AND LOVE

is not always equally exprest in the visible Effigies ; hence it happens that two of the same Nature are unlike ; the matter whereof the one consists, being lesse disposed to receive that Figure than the other ; what in that is compleat is in this imperfect'. Castiglione, too, has his doubts about the formative energy of the soul where matter is exceedingly gross and vile. 'La bellezza dell' anima . . illustra e fa bello ciò ch' ella tocca, e specialmente se quel corpo ov'ella abita non è di cosí vil materia, ch'ella non possa imprimergli la sua qualità'.[1] Spenser echoes this idea in the following lines :—

> ' —all *that faire is, is by nature good ;*
> That is a signe to know the gentle blood. [2]
> Yet oft it falles that many a gentle mynd
> Dwels in deformed tabernacle drownd,
> Either by chaunce, against the course of kynd,
> Or through *unaptnesse in the substance fownd,*
> Which it assumed of *some stubborne grownd,*
> That will not yield unto her formes direction,' [3]—

Spenser's humanism, as distinct from his scholarship, is illustrated in his view of true love and in the position given to it in his æsthetic theory. Platonists identify intellectual virtue with

[1] *Il Cortegiano*, Libro Quarto, LIX.
[2] *H. B.* st. 20.   [3] *H. B.* st. 21.

the beauty of the soul that imparts beauty to the human body. While endorsing this view, Spenser adds that true love, as opposed to 'disloiall lust',[1] also constitutes the beauty of the soul which irradiates human form. The absorption of the soul in intellect or 'its similitude to the Deity', as Plotinus has it, represents a stage of perfection which is not attainable by ordinary human beings and is not attractive to them. Its philosophy merely encourages the pursuit of a dry abstraction as celebrated in the *Hymne of Heavenly Beautie* or as emblemed forth in a different setting in Belphoebe in Book III. of the *Faerie Queene*. Spenser offers his homage to noble love between man and woman which is not based on mere intellectual culture or 'training in dialectic' purged of human connection, but is intensely human. It is this love which the amorists of the Renaissance and writers of the Italian courtesy-books of the 15th century like Castiglione and Bembo, have mentioned as a high accomplishment in courtiers and educated gentlemen. It is an ornament of the soul and the refined soul that possesses it, is sure to produce its effect on physical beauty. Spenser's idea of chastity is on a par

---

[1] *H.B.* st. 25.

## THEORIES OF BEAUTY AND LOVE 131

with this view of love. Both are inspired by humanism and prove Spenser to have been a true child of the Renaissance. He sings rapturously:

> '—*gentle Love, that loiall is and trew*,
> Will more illumine your resplendent ray,
> And adde *more brightnesse to your goodly hew*,
> From light of his pure fire:
> . .   . .   . .   . .   . .   . .
> *Therefore, to make your beautie more appeare,
> It you behoves to love*'— [1]

Beauty kindles the passion of love which also is analysed and discussed by Spenser in the manner of Plato and the Neo-Platonists. Love is described in one of his Hymns as a cosmogonic principle which unites the chaotic elements in a bond of harmony[2] and is responsible for the creation of the world.[3] Its influence also manifests itself in living creatures whose health depends on the harmonious blending (or love) of the humours in their bodies.[4] The source of this idea is, as already noted, the speech of Eryximachus in the *Symposium*. Ficinus thus dilates on it: 'Like is preserved in like. Love, however, draws like to like. Mutual love acting as the link,

---

[1] *H. B.* st. 26–27.  [2] *H. L.* st. 12.
[3] See *ante* Chapter IV.  [4] *H. L.* st. 13.

each single part of the earth is drawn to its like and is preserved in it. . . . . The parts of water draw each other alternately and are preserved through the whole body of water at a place suitable for them. The same parts of air and fire, and even these two elements, are drawn upwards by love of a region harmonious with them. . . All things, to speak the truth, are preserved by the unity of their parts and perish through their dispersion.'[1] Spenser follows Ficinus but later superimposes his own fancy on the idea of cosmogonic attraction and imagines Cupid imparting warmth to the barren cold of chaos. It is this heat that leads to procreation which is thus a means of 'quenching' the 'flame'.[2] This second type of love which is really a biological phenomenon, is attributed by Spenser to living objects—plants as well as animals. A similar conception of love as the cause of creation in the animal world is noticeable in Bembo. 'Nothing is born which does not take its birth and its origin from love as from the first and the holiest father. . . . In the moving waters male fishes, when the season comes, are followed by female fishes inspired with desire and

[1] *Commentarium in Convivium*, III. 2 quoted by L. Winstanley in her *Introduction* to the *Fowre Hymnes*, p. lx.
[2] *H. L.* st. 15.

## THEORIES OF BEAUTY AND LOVE 133

act in the way necessary for propagation, desiring the propagation of their species. Through the air the numerous birds follow one another. Likewise, wild beasts prompted by desires follow one another in their dens and thick forests and, according to one and the same eternal law, all other animals act for the love of their brief life. Not merely the sentient things cannot come into existence without love, but also the trees of the forest cannot have their roots without it. This grass on which we are now sitting and these flowers would not by their birth make the ground so beautiful and so green, if *natural love* had not united their seeds and their roots with the earth'.[1] Human love, though it is conducive to generation and perpetuation of the species, is differentiated from this *natural love* by Spenser according to whom man seeks to be immortal in his issue, while beasts have no such desire.[2] But this distinction is not authorised by Plato who ascribes love of issue and solicitude for their preservation both to man and to the beast and puts them in the same category so far as desire for immortality through reproduction is concerned.[3] Spenser mentions

[1] *Degli Asolani*, Libro II.   [2] *H.L.* st. 15.
[3] See the speech of Diotima in the *Symposium*.

another type of human love as contrasted with beastly lust. Beauty inspires this love and man's attraction for the beautiful woman is traceable to his recollection of Absolute Beauty. By loving a fair woman he only tries to possess temporarily a faint shadow of it and by begetting offspring he tries to perpetuate it in his family. Diotima says, *'Love is only birth in beauty, whether of body or of soul.* . . . There is a certain age at which human nature is desirous of procreation; and *this procreation must be in beauty* and not in deformity'. But beasts do not appreciate beauty as men always do. Following Plato, Castiglione says, 'Amor non è altro che un certo desiderio di fruir la bellezza'. Beauty is divided by this Italian Neo-Platonist into three classes which are enjoyable by man through three different faculties, viz., sense, reason and intellect. Procreation is the result of the enjoyment of some form of beauty. Romei says, 'Love is nothing else than a desire to unite with beauty and in the *Symposium,* he (Plato) says with Diotima that love is the desire to be born in beauty."[1] Romei divides human love into three kinds. The first leads the mind to the vision of

[1] *Discorsi*, Giornata Seconda.

## THEORIES OF BEAUTY AND LOVE 135

divinity, but the second type of love is less abstract and the lover 'is different from the divine lover inasmuch as in looking at human beauty he does not raise his mind to the beauty from which it proceeds, but contemplates human beauty, not as the image of divinity, but as true and essential beauty'.[1] 'The third kind of human love is that which resolves itself into a desire for union with the beautiful, not only with the soul but also with the body'. The difference between the second and the third class of Romei is not very clear, but the former seems to refer to the æsthetic appreciation of the beauty of human form, while the latter refers to the enjoyment of it through physical contact. Spenser thus refers to man's desire for possession or enjoyment of beauty in the *Hymne in Honour of Love* :—

> '— having yet in *his deducted spright*
> Some sparks remaining of that heavenly fyre,
> He is enlumind with that goodly light,
> *Unto like goodly semblant to aspyre ;*
> Therefore in choice of love he doth desyre
> That seemes on earth most heavenly to embrace,
> That same is Beautie, borne of heavenly race '.[2]

The *Phaedrus* explains the joy of the lover at the sight of beauty and contrasts it with his pangs

[1] *Discorsi*, Giornata Seconda.    [2] *H. L.* st. 16.

of separation. 'As he receives the effluence of beauty through the eyes, the wing moistens and he warms. And as he warms, the parts out of which the wing grew, and which had been hitherto closed and rigid, and had prevented the wing from shooting forth, are melted.' The result is a feeling of comfort and felicity. But when the lover is separated from his beloved, the growth of the soul's wing is arrested and the whole soul is in a state of irritation and pain. 'The soul is oppressed at the strangeness of her condition, and is in a great strait and excitement, and in her madness can neither sleep by night nor abide in her place by day. And wherever she thinks that she will behold the beautiful one, thither in her desire she runs'. Imitating Plato, Castiglione says that when a beautiful face presents itself before the lover, streams of beauty flow into the latter's heart through his eyes, heating and moistening the pores of the heart and thus liquefying the 'virtù' congealed in them. This liquid 'virtù' is then diffused round the heart where it blossoms forth and it sends out through the eyes of the lover certain vaporous 'spirits' formed of the essence of his blood.[1] When the beloved is

---

[1] *Il Cortegiano*, Libro Quarto, LXV.

## THEORIES OF BEAUTY AND LOVE    137

absent, there is no influx of beauty into the lover's heart through his eyes. Consequently its pores remain dry and cold and the 'virtù' cannot bud forth. But the memory of the beloved's beauty imparts some warmth to the lover's heart, and the 'virtù' just tries to diffuse itself. Its attempts, however, prove unsuccessful and its suppressed efforts cause to the lover misery, torment and bitterness like what children feel when first cutting teeth. These are the pangs of separation of which poets have sung and which often find expression in tears, sighs etc. '. . . . . di qua . . . . procedono le lagrime, i sospiri, gli affanni, e i tormenti degli amanti, perché l'anima sempre s'affligge e travaglia'.[1] Spenser refers, under the veil of classical imagery, to the Platonic idea of the effluence of beauty passing through the lover's eyes and imparting warmth to his heart :—

> '. . .      . . .    that imperious boy
> Doth therwith tip his sharp empoisned darts,
> Which glancing through *the eyes* with countenance coy
> Rest not till they have pierst the trembling *harts*,
> And kindled flame in all their inner parts,'—[2]

In the *Hymne in Honour of Love* the misery of

[1] *Il Cortegiano*, Libro Quarto, LXVI.    [2] *H. L.* st. 18.

lovers separated from their beloved is described in the manner of Plato and Castiglione in st. 19-20. Though the tinge of Petrarchism is undeniable in these stanzas, the reference to restless days and nights, moaning (*lagrime* in the *Cortegiano*), groans (*sospiri* in the *Cortegiano*), grieving (*tormenti* in the *Cortegiano*), etc., and the trend of the description recall the ideas of Plato and Castiglione.

Here the difference between Spenser's love-poems and the conventional Petrarchan lyric may be pointed out. The latter had of course its peculiar style and manner consisting in a copious use of puns, antitheses and conceits. Apart from this, when dealing with love and beauty, it dwelt mostly on the details of the lady's physical charms and on her heartless indifference or cruelty. Spenser's Platonism made him turn his thoughts to profounder matters and led him to explain the lover's passion and to analyse beauty as its exciting cause. From Spenser's poetry 'a consideration of beauty, as the object of love, is absent; attention is directed to the quality of the passion as one felt in the soul rather than by the sense'. Sometimes there is an 'attempt made . . . . to define love as if it were a something to be analysed—a product, as it were, of psychological

## THEORIES OF BEAUTY AND LOVE 139

elaboration'.[1] Petrarchism was also lacking in moral inspiration. 'It was as much a manner of writing sonnets as it was a method of making love'. Even where it drew upon the æsthetic theories of Plotinus, it failed to realise the beauty of moral goodness found in Spenser.

The conception of human beauty as being derived from the divine accounts for the exalted notion which the lover usually has of his beloved. The true lover not merely forms a mental image of his beloved, but also strips it of all earthly and material associations—colour, form, stature etc.— and thus forms an abstract idea of her. This idea has an affinity with his soul and it is his soul that communes with it. The formation of an idea of the beauty of the beloved is explained in the works of Italian Neo-Platonists like Pico, Benivieni and Castiglione. The *Cortegiano* gives six distinct stages of the progress of the lover, from the moment when he feels the promptings of love at the sight of a beautiful woman till the time when his soul views the wide sea of pure divine beauty. The lover first impresses her fair features upon his mind in order to alleviate the pangs of separation. Straightway, however,

[1] Harrison's *Platonism in English Poetry*, p. 149.

his imagination idealises these features and she appears to his mind to be fairer than she really is. In the second stage, it is these idealised features that the lover loves. Stimulated by the idealised beauty of the lady, he next comes to form an image of a face or figure which is, as it were, the sum of all loveliness—a combination of selected charms. In the language of Castiglione, 'besides these blessings (of beholding the lady's idealised features), the lover will find another much greater still, if he will employ this love as a step to mount to one much higher, which he will succeed in doing if he continually consider within himself how narrow a restraint it is to be always occupied in contemplating the beauty of one body only; and therefore, in order to escape such close bonds as these, in his thought he will little by little add so many ornaments that by heaping all beauties together he will form a universal concept and will reduce the multitude of these beauties to the unity of that single beauty which is spread over human nature at large. In this way he will no longer contemplate the particular beauty of one woman, but the universal beauty which adorns all bodies'.[1] When the lover is fully aware that

[1] *Il Cortegiano*, Libro Quarto.

this concept of universal beauty is primarily the product of his own mind, he realises that beauty must be an inherent part of the soul, and the passion for beauty 'growing with each fresh activity of the spirit, he now joyously contemplates beauty as he finds it within himself, quite unembarrassed by any remembrance of the senses'. Castiglione proceeds to say, 'Then the soul devoted to the contemplation of her own substance, as if awakened from deepest sleep, opens those eyes which all possess but few use, and sees in herself a ray of that light which is the true image of the angelic beauty communicated to her.' 'Now the same impulse which hitherto inclined the lover to universalise the beauty of woman, urges him to universalise that abstract beauty which he discovers within himself, and he feels out after and discovers that encircling, all-inclusive beauty of which he had before recognised but partial and subordinate manifestations. No longer does the soul contemplate beauty in her own particular intellect, but she looks forth, enraptured and ravished by its splendour, upon the vast sea of universal beauty . . . Last stage of all, the soul, burning with the sacred fire of true love and yearning to unite herself with so great beauty, actually becomes identified therewith, incorporate in the life of God'.[1] Beauty of a single woman, idealisation of this beauty, universal beauty of womankind, beauty as an attribute of the mind, intelligible beauty as an Absolute Reality, beauty of God—these are the six stages in Castiglione.

This kind of gradation of beauty is also found in the Hymns of Spenser. It has accordingly been suggested by Fletcher[2] that Spenser is the debtor of Castiglione. But Pico, writing earlier than Castiglione, had also classified beauty into six grades which appear to be similar to the six stages of Castiglione. The Sonnet of Benivieni on which Pico discoursed, also observes a similar classification of beauty. Pico writes: 'From Material Beauty we ascend to the first Fountain by six Degrees: the soul through the sight represents to herself the Beauty of some particular person, inclines to it, is pleased with it and while she rests here, is in the first, the most imperfect material degree. (2) She reforms by her imagination the image she hath received,

---

[1] *Journal of English and Germanic Philology*, Vol. XIII. p. 420.
[2] *Ibid.*, p. 418.

making it more perfect as more spiritual; and separating it from Matter, brings it a little nearer Ideal Beauty. (3) By the light of the agent Intellect abstracting this Form from all singularity, she considers the universal Nature of Corporeal Beauty by itself; this is the highest degree the Soul can reach whilest she goes no further than Sense. (4) Reflecting upon her own Operation, the knowledge of universal Beauty, and considering that everything founded in Matter is particular, she concludes this universality proceeds not from the outward object, but her Intrinsecal power; and reasons thus: If in the dimme Glasse of Material Phantasmes this beauty is represented by vertue of my Light, it follows that, beholding it in the clear Mirrour of my substance devested of those clouds, it will appear more perspicuous: thus turning into herself, she findes the Image of Ideal Beauty communicated to her by the Intellect, the Object of Celestiall Love. (5) She ascends from this Idea in her self, to the place where Celestial Venus is, in her proper form: Who in fullness of her Beauty not being comprehensible, by any particular Intellect, she, as much as in her lies, endeavours to be united to the first Minde, the chiefest of Creatures, and general Habitation of Ideal Beauty. Obtaining this, she terminates, and fixeth her journey; this is the sixth and last degree'.[1]

From a comparison of the two extracts given above, it seems very probable that Castiglione, the younger author, should have borrowed his ideas from Pico. As for Spenser's indebtedness, it is certain that he was acquainted with the works of both Pico and Castiglione and that in his Hymns he followed the Sonnet of Benivieni which was published in the same volume with Pico's commentary on it called '*A Platonick Discourse upon Love.*' Benivieni's Sonnet was a model of the poetic treatment of the sublime conception of love as elaborated by Italian Neo-Platonists. In Spenser's *Hymne in Honour of Love* only the first two stages of Pico and Castiglione find a place, while the *Hymne in Honour of Beautie* gives, in addition to these, the third and fourth stages. The first stage is easily attained. The attributing of additional charms to the beloved, involved in the second stage, is thus described by Spenser:

> ' Such is the powre of that sweet passion,
> That it all sordid basenesse doth expell,
> And the refyned *mynd doth newly fashion*
> Unto a fairer forme, which now doth *dwell*
> In his high thought—'

[1] *A Platonick Discourse upon Love*, Bk. III.

The 'fairer form' is the idealised beauty.[1] The third stage of Pico and Castiglione is the notion of universal beauty which is derived by generalisation from different specimens of earthly beauty. Here the lovers draw

> '—out of the *object of their eyes*
> *A more refyned forme, which they present*
> *Unto their mind, voide of all blemishment;*' [2]

---

[1] The germ of the idea is found in this sentence of Ficinus: 'The lover ..... has the power of beholding in the beloved the true and original nature and therefore of constructing in his mind's eye the ethereal form which is far more beautiful; it is this image which he always sees and this image which he loves, and therefore lovers so often believe each other far more beautiful than they are'. Castiglione gives a detailed description of the process of formation of the image of the ideal beauty of the beloved and distinguishes the different parts played in it by the eye, the heart and the imagination. The 'virtù' liquefied by the streams of beauty flowing into the lover's heart through his eyes, blossoms forth and sends out through these eyes certain vaporous spirits formed of the essence of his blood. These meet the beloved and invest her with all sorts of imaginary charms (*Il Cortegiano*, Libro Quarto, LXV). Bembo means much the same thing when he says, ' Lovers go with their sight to every place and for what appears they see easily the other things which remain hidden, because, my dear ladies, you conceal within your breast from other men what you can which you can't keep concealed from the lovers. And then Perottino will say that lovers are blind; but he is blind who does not see things that are to be seen.' (*Degli Asolani*, Libro II).

[2] *H. B.* st. 31.

and this the *mind*
> 'Beholdeth *free from fleshes frayle infection.*'

In the fourth stage, the lover realises beauty purely as a spiritual entity and as an inherent part of his soul. The beauty which 'he fashions in his higher skill' he admires as *'the mirrour of his owne thought'*
> 'Which seeing now so *inly faire to be*,
> As outward it appeareth to the eye,
> And with *his spirits proportion to agree*,
> He thereon fixeth all his fantasie,'—[1]

The last two stages of Pico and Castiglione are taken up in the Hymns to Heavenly Love and Heavenly Beauty and will be considered later.

The stages of progress of the lover in Spenser resemble the grades of the soul's ascent in the course of its heavenward flight in Benivieni's Sonnet entitled the *Ode of Love*. The number of the grades in Benivieni is not six and the last grades in the *Ode of Love* are not dealt with by Spenser in his Hymns to Beauty and Love. These grades, roughly corresponding to the last

---

[1] *H. B.* st. 33. Kinship of nature between lovers is also referred to in Romei. 'Love is not possible until a woman is found whose beauty conforms to his (i.e., the lover's) own nature. This occult conformity is one of the principal and essential causes of love which has its origin in nothing else than the celestial influences in the generation of man.' (*Discorsi*, Giornata Seconda.)

## THEORIES OF BEAUTY AND LOVE 147

two stages in Pico and Castiglione, represent a plane partially reached in the Hymns to Heavenly Love and Heavenly Beauty. Benivieni broadly divides the soul's upward march into three grades represented by three[1] forms of beauty—viz., of the body, of the heart and of the mind or intellect. There are, however, sub-divisions of each of these grades. Though there is no strict correspondence amongst the grades and sub-grades of Benivieni and the stages of Pico, Castiglione and Spenser, some resemblance amongst them is, indeed, clearly discernible. The idealised beauty of the beloved reached in the second stage of the lover's progress in Pico and in Castiglione and called by Spenser 'a fairer forme',[2] is referred to by Benivieni when he describes the apprehension of beauty by the heart in these lines :

> '—first the eyes, next through these whence sojourns
> Its other handmaid, does *the heart embrace*
> *That fairness, though less base,*
> *Not full expressed—*'

The idea of universal beauty represented by the third stage of Pico and of Castiglione and referred to by Spenser in stanza 31 of the *Hymne in*

[1] *Ode of Love*, st. 7.   [2] *H. L.* st. 28.

## 148   PLATONIC IDEAS IN SPENSER

*Honour of Beautie,* appears in the following lines of Benivieni :—

> '. . . from many fairs
> The *heart from matter tears,*
> Is shaped *a type, wherein what nature rends
> In all asunder, into one there blends* '.[1]

Beauty as an inherent attribute of the mind, comprehensible by the intellect alone, which is the subject-matter of the lover's experience in the fourth stage according to Pico and Castiglione and is referred to by Spenser as 'the mirrour of his owne thought' in st. 32 of the *Hymne in Honour of Beautie,* is suggested in stanza 8 of the *Ode of Love* in these two lines :—

> ' If gentle heart those sacred signs pursue,
> It finds that image planted in the mind '—

The lover may be deemed to enjoy the product of his own mind when he idealises the beauty of his beloved as much as when he perceives it as part of his own mind or soul. Ordinary people would be inclined to look upon an advanced lover of this type as a prey to his own fervid imagination. Spenser declares that such a lover sees 'more then any other eyes can see'.[2]   In stanza 6 of his *Ode*

---

[1] *Ode of Love*, st. 7.    [2] *H. B.* st. 34.

## THEORIES OF BEAUTY AND LOVE 149

*of Love,* Benivieni describes him as feeding on a 'sweet error'. Again, in stanza 7 he repeats,

> 'On a *sweet error* the heart feeds, its dear
> One deeming that which of itself was born'.[1]

Spenser has followed Plato in the *Hymne in Honour of Love* on some other points also. His statements that love is born of Plenty and Penury and that he is at once the eldest and the youngest of the gods, have been traced to Plato ultimately. Both have been explained by Pico in his *Discourse;* but the second, as pointed out in the *Cambridge History of English Literature*[2] and by Miss Winstanley,[3] is directly borrowed from Ficinus who tried to reconcile the speeches of Phaedrus and Agathon in the *Symposium.*

---

[1] Shakespeare looks upon this idealising tendency of the lover, which invests his beloved with imaginary charms and graces as equivalent to a madman's fantasy. He writes:
> 'Lovers and madmen have such seething brains,
> Such *shaping fantasies, that apprehend*
> More than *cool reason ever comprehends.*
> . . . . . . . . . . . . . . . the lover . . .
> *Sees Helen's beauty in a brow of Egypt'*—
> (*A Midsummer Night's Dream*, Act V. Sc. I.)

[2] Vol. III. p. 216.
[3] Notes to *Hymn* I. p. 45.

## CHAPTER VI

### HEAVENLY LOVE—BLENDING OF NEO-PLATONISM AND CHRISTIAN THEOLOGY

SPENSER distinguishes Heavenly Love from earthly love which he calls a 'mad fit' and on which he had written profusely in his youth.[1] Recognition of this contrast is common enough. Spenser's conception of Heavenly Love has, however, some special features which are the outcome of a combination of Neo-Platonic philosophy and Christian theology.

Heavenly Love, as generally conceived in English poetry of the 16th and 17th centuries, is love felt by God Himself and manifested in His creation of the world. The metaphysical basis of this conception was supplied by the Neo-Platonism of Plotinus which traces the evolution of the world from the ultimate Reality through distinct stages. This Reality is called the One, Beauty or the Good and is indescribable, inconceivable and beyond rational comprehension. The Intellect which emanates from the One is

[1] *H. H. L.* st. 2.

dual, involving consciousness of the distinction between subject and object. The Soul which emanates from the Intellect is multiform. These three entities possess different types of beauty. The philosophical trinity of Plotinus received various interpretations and during the Renaissance Ficinus identified the One with the Christian idea of God and put a Platonic interpretation on the emanation-theory of Plotinus. The Highest Reality, according to Plato, is Absolute Beauty. 'In the *Symposium* Plato had taught that love was a desire of birth in beauty, and that the highest love was a desire of birth in beauty absolute, the ultimate principle of all beauty. Christianity, on the other hand, had taught that God is love. By identifying the absolute beauty of Plato with God, and by applying the Platonic conception of the birth of love to this Christian conception of God as love, God Himself was understood as enjoying His own beauty, thus begetting beings like to it in fairness'.[1] The issue of God's love (of His own beauty) is the Son, while from the union of God and the Son is derived the third person of the Trinity. The beauty of the last two persons of the Trinity is inferior to God's and their

---

[1] Harrison's *Platonism in English Poetry*, p. 68.

essence too is less spiritual than His. They were identified with the Intellect and the Soul, the second and third emanations of Plotinus. Commenting on Bk. V. of *Ennead* III. of Plotinus, Ficinus says, 'The first Intellect, God's, which is pure intellect, is most foreign to matter. Moreover, we conclude that the *intelligent* soul, *directly created* by that First Intelligence, God, and, therefore, intellectual in the highest degree, cannot be united to matter so as to have the common form of one composite, for this intellectual soul is indeed Intelligence; the life that springs from this union (between God and Intelligence) is, so to say, a soul, simply, a nature which can now be united with matter. Hence that Intellectual soul in the world we call the *first reproductive principle,* the life further infused into the world we call the *second reproductive principle*. In both there exists a *perpetual love for the beauty of the divine mind'*.[1] 'The desire of propagating oneself is love in a certain sense. Absolute perfection is in the highest power of God. Divine Intelligence contemplates it (perfection) and hence feels a desire to propagate beyond and outside itself. From this

---

[1] *Plotini Divini illius è Platonica familia Philosophi De rebus Philosophicis*, Lib. LIII.

## HEAVENLY LOVE

love of propagation all things are created. For this reason Dionysius said that Love did not permit the Ruler of all things to contain Himself in Himself without offspring'.[1] Plotinus' three philosophical principles are also expressly identified by Ficinus in his commentary with the three hypostases of the Christian Trinity. He says, 'Plotinus, indeed, after Plato, supposes that the Intellectual soul, when it thinks of God and tries to understand Him and to long for Him, conceives within itself not something quite imaginary, but a subsistent reality. In this Plotinus had before his mind, I suppose, the *mystery of the Christian Trinity*'.

Spenser[2] borrowed his complex and striking conception of Heavenly Love with its Christian colouring from Ficinus' Christian interpretation of the emanation-theory of Neo-Platonism. It was not an original conception of Spenser or of other English poets of the 16th and 17th centuries, as suggested by Harrison.[3] Traces of this inter-

---

[1] *Commentarium in Convivium*, III. 2 quoted by L. Winstanley. See her *Introduction* to the *Fowre Hymnes*, p. lx.

[2] Attempts to identify the three Plotinian principles with the Christian Trinity are also noticeable in Henry More and Drummond.

[3] *Platonism in English Poetry*, p. 67.

pretation are also to be found in Pico. Pico admits that God from eternity produced a creature of incorporeal and *intellectual* nature, but he would call it, along with Plato and others, 'the Daughter of God, the *Minde, Wisdom,* not meaning (with our Divines) the Son of God, he not being a creature'.[1] Following the teachings of Ficinus, Spenser in the *Hymne of Heavenly Love* sings of God's love of Himself, the birth of His Son[2] and the birth of the 'most holy, most almightie Spright',[3] the third person of the Christian Trinity. But the poet makes additions to, and alterations in, the teachings of the Italian Neo-Platonist, mentions angels as 'His second brood'[4] and also refers to man as being 'made by love out of His owne like mould',[5] though 'of clay, base, vile, and next to nought'.[6]

Spenser's Calvinism, however, is responsible for many of his deviations from the philosophy of Plotinus. For example, in Spenser the Son, though His creation[7] by God is expressly referred to, is not in any way inferior to the Father, but equal to Him in dignity. He is 'the firstling of his

---

[1] *A Platonick Discourse upon Love*, Bk. I. Sec. IV.
[2] *H. H. L.* st. 5.   [3] *H. H. L.* st. 6.
[4] *Ibid.* st. 8.   [5] *Ibid.* st. 17.
[6] *Ibid.* st. 16.   [7] *Ibid.* st. 5.

joy . . whom he therefore with *equall honour crownd*'.[1] In Plotinus, however, the second entity is appreciably inferior to the One in essence as well as in beauty. Further, the Soul in Plotinus is an emanation from the Intellect : the multiform issues out of the biform. But Spenser derives his 'third' from both the Father and the Son.

> ' With him he raignd, before all time prescribed,
> In endlesse glorie and immortall might,
> Together with that third *from them derived*,
> Most wise, most holy, most almightie Spright ! '

This is in strict accordance with Calvin's theology.[2] The third person of the Trinity has also been given in Spenser a position equal to that of the Father in accordance with the doctrine of Calvin, whereas in Plotinus the third entity or the Soul is distinctly inferior to the first as also to the second. The Soul is also not beyond human comprehension in Plotinus as the Holy Spirit is represented[3] to be in Spenser. In the *Hymne of Heavenly Love* Spenser's ideas seem to bear some resemblance to the theories of 'Christianised Neo-Platonism which culminated in the ninth century, when Joannes Scotus (Erigena) popularised the doctrines of the so-called Dionysius the Areopagite.'

[1] *H. H. L.* st. 5.   [2] *Modern Philology*, Vol. XII. p. 3.
[3] *H. H. L.* st. 6, last lines.

There is a second form of Heavenly Love celebrated in the third Hymn of Spenser. It is a strictly Christian conception and means God's infinite affection and mercy as manifested in the means provided by Him for the expiation of man's sins and his redemption. It is an ideal of moral perfection as distinguished from the first kind of Heavenly Love described above which is based on a metaphysical theory. Spenser thus refers to it :—

> '. . . that great Lord of Love, which him at first
> Made of meere love, and after liked well,
> Seeing him lie like creature long accurst
> In that deepe horror of despeyred hell,
> Him, wretch, in doole would let no lenger dwell,
> But cast out of that bondage to redeeme,
> And pay the price, all were his debt extreeme '.[1]

The idea underlying this stanza has exact parallels in these passages from the Bible : 'Hereby perceive we the *love of God,* because he laid down his life for us : and we ought to lay down *our* lives for the brethren'.[2] 'Herein is love, not that we loved God, but that he loved us, and sent his Son to be the propitiation for our sins'.[3]

The third form of Heavenly Love in Spenser is really similar to the second, though it is repre-

---

[1] *H. H. L.* st. 19.   [2] 1 John III. 16.
[3] 1 John IV. 10.

sented in the third Hymn not as an attribute of God Himself (as the other two forms are), but as a moral ideal to be attained by a true Christian. It signifies moral purity and goodness in man which make his communion with God possible and refers to the Redemptive Love of God typified in Christ as the ideal to be followed by him.

It is this type of Heavenly Love which Spenser distinguishes from earthly love or 'mad fit' in st. 2 of the third hymn. This refined love is to supplant man's desire for worldly things wherein lies moral degradation and it has its beginnings in our love of human beings as our brothers.[1] The Greeks had insisted on intellectual and æsthetic culture as the goal of human life, which is signified in Plato's teaching that Wisdom or Beauty is the supreme Reality; but Christianity laid stress on moral Perfection as the 'summum bonum' of human existence and conceived of God as a Moral Ideal. The *Hymne of Heavenly Beautie* is based on the Greek view, and the love of Sapience or Wisdom which is its subject-matter, is *amor intellectualis* of the Greeks and may be called the fourth kind of Heavenly Love in Spenser, while the third

---

[1] *H.H.L.* st. 29.

Hymn sings of the Christian Ideal of (moral) Perfection typified in the life of Christ Himself.

Though this ideal is Christian, Spenser's Platonism comes out in the means recommended by him for its realisation. This is modelled on the progression in æsthetic and intellectual culture as explained in the *Symposium* and the *Republic,* in which the lower stage (of beauty) leads up to the higher and more abstract stage till the highest is reached. Applying this (dialectical) process to Christian training, Spenser makes the successive stages of advance consist, first, of the visualization of the different episodes of Christ's life ending with His self-immolation for the Redemption of man and next, of meditation on its various spiritual aspects. The poet first refers to the tortures inflicted on Christ—the mangling of His body, the 'bitter wounds' on His hands[1] and feet, etc.—as a spectacle to move the eye, but later he asks people to lift up their minds and meditate upon 'his endlesse merit'.[2] Spenser's strong Calvinism here makes him insist on their further purification and he asks them to give themselves up 'full and free' to Him and to beg for His Grace. And

[1] *H.H.L.* st. 35.     [2] *H.H.L.* st. 37.

when this stage of purification is over, the ravished soul has a sight not of

'his most sacred heavenly corse',[1]

but of the very

' Idee of his pure glorie'.[2]

Contemplation of the moral life of Christ is thus rewarded with the realisation of His Divine nature. In other words, the man-Christ leads the soul to God-Christ or 'Christ as God sees him, Christ as an aspect of Divinity and as merged in Him'.[3] This sublimation of the love of Christ's earthly body into the love of His Divine nature has been described as an antidote to erotic mysticism. There was a strong tendency, says Harrison, in the religious poetry of the 16th and 17th centuries towards a phase of devotional love the object of which was Christ conceived as the perfection of physical beauty. 'The spectacle of the crucified Saviour of man was especially influential in keeping this strain of mystical devotion alive ; and the minds of these poets are continually dwelling upon the beauty of

[1] *H.H.L.* st. 36.  [2] *H.H.L.* st. 41.
[3] *Journal of English and Germanic Philology*, Vol. XIII. p. 424 and *Modern Philology*, Vol. VIII. p. 546.

his mangled hands and feet . . . . The first way by which this elevation of a purely sensuous passion into a higher region was effected was through the Platonic conception of the "Idea".' 'Whenever Platonism enters into this tender passion, it always elevates the emotion into a higher region where the more intellectual or spiritual nature of Christ or God is the object of contemplation . . . as a philosophical principle, whether of beauty, of good, or of true being."[1]

The first kind of Heavenly Love based on the metaphysics of Plato and Plotinus but with a tinge of Christian Theology in it, has already been differentiated from the third which is essentially a Christian idea, though Spenser's handling of it is Platonic. The first symbolises the evolution of the world from the one ultimate Reality, described by Plotinus as emanation. The third kind of Heavenly Love is depicted as the ascent of the soul till it is merged in God-Christ or the Divine Idea. This progression is a Platonic idea, and emanation in Plotinus is only the counter-process of Platonic progression. Emanation and absorption follow each other as the day does the night, and Neo-Platonism sees in this ceaseless cosmic

---

[1] *Platonism in English Poetry*, pp. 93–95.

## HEAVENLY LOVE

operation the proper exercise of Divine energy. The poetical handling of this topic in Spenser has a parallel in Benivieni's *Ode of Love* which traces the progress of the soul's journey from its descent on the earth to its return to its Divine source.[1]

The difference between Benivieni and Spenser is that the former deals with the Neo-Platonic theme as a purely philosophic conception, while the latter modifies it through the introduction of Christian forms of thought.

[1] 'I tell how Love from its celestial source
In primal Good flows to the world of sense;
When it had birth, and whence,
That moves the heavens, refines the soul, gives laws
To all; in men's hearts taking residence,
With what arms keen and ready in resource,
It is the gracious force
Which mortal minds from earth to heaven draws;'—
(*Ode of Love*, st. 2.)

# CHAPTER VII

## MYSTICISM—HEAVENLY BEAUTY

SPENSER conceives of Heavenly Beauty as the attribute of an immaterial entity which is called Sapience and differentiates it from sensible beauty which is an attribute of material substance. Ordinary physical beauty can be apprehended by sense and described in language; but, for the realisation of Heavenly Beauty, the help not of the eye but of the mind or of contemplation is necessary. He says in the *Hymne of Heavenly Beautie,*

> '. . . gathering plumes of perfect speculation,
> To impe the wings of thy *high flying mynd,*
> Mount up aloft *through heavenly contemplation,*
> From this darke world, whose damps the soule do blynd,
> And, like the native brood of Eagles kynd,
> On that bright Sunne of Glorie fixe thine eyes'—[1]

To assert, however, that Heavenly Beauty has to be apprehended by the mind, is not an adequate description of its nature—it is the beauty of the mind or intellect itself. This beauty can be divided into two forms. In one form it is beauty apprehended as part of the mind of the perceiver. Here it is the beauty of the individual intellect.

[1] *H.H.B.* st. 20.

The second form of intellectual beauty is more comprehensive than the possession of any individual mind and is to be realised as universal beauty. Beyond these two forms is the third form of beauty—sometimes called the beauty of God—which transcends perception and intellection and can only be realised through direct communion. A rough, but somewhat similar, classification of intellectual beauty is to be found in Plato. Diotima says in the *Symposium,* 'The true order of going, or being led by another, to the things of love, is to use the beauties of earth as steps along which he mounts upwards for the sake of that other beauty, going from one to two, and from two to all fair forms, and from fair forms to fair actions, and from fair actions to fair notions, until from fair notions he arrives at the notion of absolute beauty, and at last knows what the essence of beauty is'. Here 'fair notions', 'notion of absolute beauty' and 'the essence of beauty' mean respectively the first, the second and the third form of intellectual or spiritual beauty as described above. The 'abundance of beauty' which is distinguished from 'the beauty of one youth, or man or institution' and the 'single science which is the science of beauty everywhere', mentioned as the last two rungs of the famous ladder of ascent in the *Symposium,* seem to stand for the second and third forms of beauty as classified above, i.e., universal beauty and the beauty of God. Again, in the *Phaedrus,* the 'being' or 'true knowledge' seen by the winged soul during its heavenward flight, may typify the second or the third form of intellectual beauty. Plotinus clearly distinguishes the beauty of God from that of the most universal truth—the beauty of the One from that of the Intellect or Nous. It has already[1] been pointed out how the lover in Pico and in Castiglione reaches his goal through the progressive realisation of six forms of beauty. The last three can be identified with the three kinds of beauty mentioned above. Thus their fourth stage is the beauty of the particular mind—Truth *'sub specie temporis'* as distinguished from Truth *'sub specie aeternitatis'*[2] represented by their fifth grade which is universal beauty or the beauty of universal Truth. Spenser has dealt with the first four stages of Pico and Castiglione, including Truth *sub specie temporis,* in his first two Hymns.[3] He

---

[1] See *ante* Chapter V.
[2] *Modern Philology,* Vol. VIII. p. 552.
[3] For a pointed contrast between physical beauty and beauty of the individual mind or truth '*sub specie temporis,*' see the *Epithalamion.*

takes up universal beauty or Truth *'sub specie aeternitatis'* in his *Hymne of Heavenly Beautie*. Owing to his strict Calvinism which condemns man's boldness in trying to approach God directly, Spenser refrains from describing Divine beauty and conceives of Heavenly Beauty not as the beauty of God, but that of Universal Truth or Sapience (referred to in the *Phaedrus* of Plato). Sapience is represented by him as the beloved of God sitting on His very bosom.[1] According to Christian theology, Sapience stands for *Logos*, the mind of God, as distinguished from His Redemptive Love which is figured forth in Christ and dealt with in Spenser's *Hymne of Heavenly Love*. The representation of Sapience as a feminine being beloved of God is, however, due to Gnostic influence.[2]

Reference[3] has already been made to Benivieni's *Ode of Love* which deals with the various grades of beauty rising up to the beauty of the individual mind. The poem also goes on to describe abstract or universal beauty (the fifth stage of Pico and of Castiglione) represented in Spenser's Hymn by Sapience. The image implanted in the mind, as

[1] *H.H.B.* st. 27.
[2] *Modern Philology*, Vol. VIII. p. 546.
[3] See *ante* Chapter V.

set forth in st. 8 of the *Ode of Love,* is a step of ascent leading to the beauty that imparts grace to everything in this world and hence is called universal beauty. Benivieni, like Spenser, shrinks from the next step,—from coming face to face with the beauty of God.

For the notion of Heavenly Beauty Spenser is indebted to Plato as much as to the Neo-Platonists; but the method of its progressive realisation is borrowed by him directly from the *Symposium.* This method had been used by some of the Neo-Platonists and by Spenser himself in his *Hymne of Heavenly Love.*[1] Spenser argues in his fourth Hymn that the sea which encircles the earth is more beautiful than the latter and the stars farther off are fairer than the sea.[2] The firmament—'that mightie shining christall wall'—is, again, finer than the stars, the 'pyles of flaming brands'. On these facts supplied by the Lucretian cosmology, Spenser formulates the theory that material objects are beautiful in proportion as they are physically distant from this gross earth and extends its application first to the Ptolemaic universe, next to the habitation of the Platonic 'Idees' beyond it and lastly to the abode of the

---

[1] See *ante* Chapter VI.  [2] *H.H.B.* st. 6–14.

Powers, Potentates, Princes and Dominations of the Christian Hierarchy. The poet mounts up on the stepping-stones of these celestial bodies in the hope of seeing Heavenly Beauty at last in the highest heavens; but it remains unseen. For, though use has been made of a ladder of ascent, the progression has not been from the concrete to the abstract as recommended in the *Symposium*, but from the nearer to the more distant. The difference in respect of beauty between one celestial body and another is consequently one of degree, and not of kind as in Plato; and the vision of the different stages of beauty does not involve the gradual purgation of sense-impression necessary for realising the beauty of Sapience which is essentially different in kind from the finest specimen of physical beauty in the most ethereal region. Spenser has, therefore, to admit the failure of his upward march which is incapable of[1] giving any impression of the 'essentiall parts' of Heavenly Beauty. He makes a second attempt. This time also he begins with images of physical beauty but, following the teaching of Diotima, he now uses them (with the help of the *intellect*) merely as a means to the realisation of beauty of a higher and

[1] *H.H.B.* st. 16.

more abstract type, viz., the beauty of spiritual and intellectual qualities—of God's wisdom and goodness as displayed in His Creation—and, by a gradual progress along the new path, arrives at the most abstract hypostasis—Heavenly Beauty or Sapience.[1]

The idea of a hierarchy of heavenly bodies with increasing degrees of brilliance was prevalent in Europe when astronomical knowledge was crude. Plato's suggestion about the existence of an intelligible world, perfect and resplendent,[2] and his theory of Absolute Beauty imparting loveliness and lustre to other objects, probably lent some support to this idea during the Renaissance. Bembo describes the arrangement of different regions in the heavens, one above another, according to the fineness of their substance and their brilliance—e.g., this world, the stars, pure element, firmament filled with air, etc. Bembo also believes that another world—the world of ideas—'most divine, most intelligible, most illuminated and itself becoming better and greater as much as it nears itself to the Final Cause', really exists above these celestial bodies.[3] In explaining the nature of Sapience or Heavenly Beauty,

[1] *Phaedo*, 110–111. [2] *H.H.B.* st. 12.
[3] *Degli Asolani*, Libro III.

by critics 'traditional Platonism'[1] in his last two Hymns (as well as a slight mystic tinge in Bk. I. of the *Faerie Queene*). In one sense, Platonism is akin to mysticism and 'Plato is, after all, the father of European mysticism'. But Plato does not enunciate any canon and mysticism does not appear in him in a very pronounced form. Mysticism is more prominent in Plotinus and 'for the mediaeval mystics Platonism meant the philosophy of Plotinus adapted by Augustine'.[2] Plotinus was the great source of mysticism in Italy during the Renaissance and his mysticism lent colour to the theories of love popularised by the Italian Neo-Platonists. Pico's *Discourse* and Benivieni's *Ode of Love* illustrate this mysticism based on the Platonic tradition which is also noticeable in Spenser.

The creeds of mysticism have been aptly summarized by Dean Inge. Its first creed is that the inner being in man has a distinct faculty for the apprehension of the Divine. As Inge puts it, 'We have an organ or faculty for the discernment of spiritual truth, which, in its proper sphere, is as much to be trusted as the organs of sensation

---

[1] 'Platonism in English Poetry' in *English Literature and the Classics*, p. 27.
[2] Inge's *Christian Mysticism*, p. 78.

in theirs'.[1] Mystic apprehension of the supreme Reality is as vivid as, or even more vivid than, sense-perception and rational comprehension. It is, however, frequently described as a vision; for sight seems to man to be the most vivid and the most reliable form of perception. In the *Phaedrus* as well as in the *Symposium,* the Supreme Reality is described as *an object of vision.* Plotinus says, 'The perception of the highest God is not effected by science nor by intelligence. . . . But the *vision of him* is now the work of one solicitous to perceive Him.' In Spenser's fourth Hymn also the perception of the Heavenly Beauty of Sapience is figured as a *vision.* The poet says :—

' Let Angels, which her *goodly face behold*
And see at will, her soveraigne praises sing,'—[2]

The second proposition of mysticism is that man, 'in order to know God, must be a partaker of the divine nature'.[3] Communion between two things is based on their similarity which furnishes points of contact between them. Communion between

[1] Inge's *Christian Mysticism*, p. 6.
[2] *H.H.B.*, st. 34.
[3] Inge's *Christian Mysticism*, p. 78.

the human soul and God which is emblemed as a vision, is possible only when the former becomes consubstantial with the latter—the perceiver with the object of vision. Thus the spiritual in man must separate itself from the trammels of sense in order to have contact with the ultimate Reality. Says Plotinus, 'The sensitive eye can never be able to survey the orb of the sun, unless strongly endowed with solar fire and participating largely of the vivid ray. Every one therefore must become divine, and of godlike beauty, before he can gaze upon a God and the beautiful itself'. Hence in the *Hymne of Heavenly Love* Spenser begs of *Love to lift him up,* so that he might have a vision of Heavenly Love.[1] Man's soul must be full of love before communion with the God of Love is possible. Here the communion is a moral ideal in consonance with the teachings of Christianity and is the result of man's attainment of moral similitude to the Son of God. But the Greek conception of Intellectual culture as making man consubstantial with Universal Truth or Wisdom, underlies the poet's invocation to Truth in the *Hymne of Heavenly Beautie* :

---

[1] *H.H.L.* st. 1.

> 'Vouchsafe then, O thou most Almightie Spright!
> From whom all guifts of *wit and knowledge* flow,
> To shed into my breast some sparkling light
> Of thine *eternall Truth*, that I may show
> Some litle beames to mortall eyes below—'[1]

Benivieni expresses a similar idea in the first stanza of his *Ode of Love* and though he uses the word 'love', the reference is not to the moral ideal exclusively. He says:

> 'Love, from whose hands suspended hang the reins
> Unto my heart, who in his high empire
> Scorns *not to feed the fire*
> *By him enkindled in me long ago,*
> Would move my tongue, my faculties inspire
> To tell what my enamoured breast retains
> Of him . . .'

Union of two consubstantial things is only natural. Strictly speaking, a vision presupposes the existence of the beholder and the beheld, i.e., of two separate things; and it is clearly impossible where the two become one. But mystic vision is only another name for the merging of the one in the other. Of this final union of consubstantial things, Plotinus says, 'Perhaps, however, neither must it be said that he sees, but that he is the thing seen; if it is necessary to call these two

---

[1] *H.H.B.* st. 2.

things, i.e., the perceiver and the thing perceived. But *both are one;* though it is bold to assert this. . . . Since, therefore, (in this conjunction with deity), there were not two things, but the perceiver was one with the thing perceived, as *not being (properly speaking) vision but union*'.[1] Pico also says that the highest Reality is reached only when the soul is transformed into and merged in it. 'This is the Image of Celestial Love, by which Man ariseth from one perfection to another, till his Soul is made an Angel. Purged from Material dross and transformed into spiritual flame by this Divine Power, he mounts up to the Intelligible Heaven, and happily rests in his Father's bosome'.[2] According to Spenser, when there is communion between human beings and Heavenly Beauty, the latter

'. . . . . . doth bereave
Their soule of sense, through infinite delight,
And them transport from flesh into the spright.' [3]

The 8th stanza of Benivieni's *Ode of Love* deals with this idea of consubstantiation of the human soul with the Primal Essence in which it is ultimately merged.

---

[1] Plotinus on the Good, or the One ; *Enneads*, VI. ix.
[2] Pico's *Discourse*.      [3] *H.H.B.* st. 37.

'The soul thus entring in the Minde,
There such uncertainty doth finde,
*That she to clearer Light applies
Her Armes, and near the first Sun flies.* [1]

[1] Stanley's Translation.

## CHAPTER VIII

### THE *AMORETTI*—NEO-PLATONISM THROUGH FRENCH SONNETEERS

THE debt of the Elizabethan sonnet to foreign literatures has been pointed out in detail by Sir Sidney Lee.[1] In England sonneteering was at first inspired by the example of Petrarch whose work was imitated copiously by Wyatt and Surrey. After Surrey's death in 1547, there followed a barren quarter of a century and when, at the close of it, the sonnet reappeared in English Literature, the impulse came from the activities of the French sonneteers, especially of the Pléiade, though 'throughout the same epoch Italian Literature was still bearing rich fruit, and it was Italian literary energy that dominated the new French outburst.' After the sonnet had been re-introduced from France, however, 'Petrarch quickly reasserted over the Elizabethan sonnet that supremacy which Wyatt and Surrey had acknowledged'.[2] Yet the best Elizabethan sonneteers of the later period, steeped as they were in Petrarchism, studied thoroughly the writings

[1] See the *Introduction* to his *Elizabethan Sonnets*.
[2] Lee's *Introduction*, p. xxxiii.

## 178   PLATONIC IDEAS IN SPENSER

of the Pléiade masters, while the inferior ones concentrated their attention on contemporary France alone—they even derived their knowledge of Petrarch and his Italian followers from the French adaptations of Italian sonnets. The extent of the French influence on Spenser in this respect may be gauged from the fact that Spenser, as observed by Sir Sidney Lee, passed to the study of Italian through the study of French. The evidence of young Spenser's love of French is furnished by the poet's early translations[1] (in the sonnet form) of Du Bellay's French sonnets, to which were subsequently added translations of Du Bellay's longer series of sonnets, *Les Antiquités de Rome,* and of Marot's twelve-lined stanzas entitled *Les Visions de Petrarque.*[2] Subsequently, notes Sir Sidney Lee, Spenser read Petrarch 'in the Italian text, and at a much later date, devised a new sonnet-sequence on the Petrarchan plan'. On the whole, his obligation to Petrarch, though commencing later, is not negligible in the *Amoretti.*[3] Yet, besides Spenser's early translations of Du Bellay and Marot, the *Amoretti* show also his interest in,

---

[1] Under the title of *The Visions of Bellay.*
[2] French translation of an ode of Petrarch.
[3] See Lee's *Introduction,* p. xciv and *Modern Language Review,* Vol. XXII. pp. 194–5.

and obligation to, French sonneteers of the sixteenth century. Though Spenser was not guilty of wholesale literary piracy like some other noted Elizabethans, his debt to the French sonnet is remarkable.[1] Critics have pointed out the resemblance between Spenser's sonnets and their French models in respect of their language and imagery; but the Platonism of the *Amoretti* also has its source, in one sense, in the productions of the Platonising sonneteers of France of the 16th century, notably of the Pléiade, and the form in which Platonic ideas appear in some of the *Amoretti* sonnets and the manner in which they have been woven into the structure of the poems, point to the influence of the French masters.

Petrarch's sonnets, like Dante's, are said to be dominated by the Platonic ideal of love.[2] Symonds, however, draws a distinction between Laura and Beatrice. The latter 'passed from the sphere of the human into the divine; and though her face was still beautiful, it was the face of Science rather than of one we love'. Laura, on the other hand, says Symonds, 'stands midway between the Beatrice of Dante and the women of

[1] See *Modern Language Review*, Vol. IV. pp. 67–69 and Lee's *Introduction*, p. xcv *et seq.*
[2] See Lee's *Introduction*, p. xv.

Boccaccio. She is not so much a woman with a character and personality, as woman in the general, *la femme,* personified and made the object of a poet's reveries."[1] Petrarch's conception of love, such as it is, has been overshadowed by his literary art and his peculiar conceits to which his followers turned with facility for imitation. The intellectual and spiritual note of Petrarch, however, is not to be found in any of those sonnets of Spenser in which scholars have discovered the influence of the Petrarchan model, e.g., sonnets numbered 12, 16, 25, 36 and 57 of the *Amoretti.* These merely reproduce the common Petrarchan conceits and copy the Petrarchan style in describing the physical charms of the lady, her varying moods, her cruelty, her tyranny, etc. For the source of Platonism in the *Amoretti,* an examination of the works of the French sonneteers of the sixteenth century, especially of the Pléiade, is more fruitful.

Platonism was the dominant note of French poetry from 1540 to 1550 and it was encouraged by Margaret of Navarre. Bonaventure Despériers[2] was entrusted with the translation of Plato's *Lysis.* The school of Lyons, with Maurice Scève

---

[1] See *Renaissance in Italy*, Vol. IV. pp. 77, 81.
[2] 1500–1544.

as its chief, gave considerable impetus to the study of Platonism, but being nearer to Italy, it followed Italian models in the treatment of love. Petrarchism and Renaissance Neo-Platonism were combined in Scève. Héroët, though of the same school, in his chief work *La Parfaite Amye* (1542) developed the idea of love in the light of the discourses of Castiglione and Ficinus and repudiated Petrarchism as distinct from Platonism.[1] Later Pontus de Thyard also added to the stream of Platonism in France by his translation of the *Dialoghi d' Amore* of the Spanish Jew Leo Hebræus. The effect of all this interest in Italian Neo-Platonism in France can be noticed in the sonnets of Ronsard and his followers and 'it is worthy of note also that several of the gems of Pléiade verse owe their inspiration to the lofty conception of Platonism, the theme par-excellence of the almost forgotten poetry which immediately preceded the work of Ronsard and his friends,' though, as has been pointed out, the interest of Ronsard, Du Bellay and Pontus de Thyard in Platonism was short-lived, while some other members of the Pléiade were hostile to Plato's philosophy of love and beauty as expounded by

[1] *Modern Philology*, Vol. V. p. 415.

## 182   PLATONIC IDEAS IN SPENSER

Castiglione and Héroët. The most striking feature of this exposition is the gradation of beauty in accordance with the different stages of the lover's progress in his upward march.[1] Some sonnets of the Pléiade show that this exposition of Plato's ideas was availed of by the French sonneteers and their obligation to the Italian treatises of Castiglione and Pico or to works based on them, like those of Héroët, is not merely conjectural. Though not members of the Pléiade, Desportes and Claude de Pontoux also imbibed a taste for Italian Neo-Platonism which is manifested in their sonnets. Spenser's *Amoretti,* besides imitating the language of some of the French sonnets of this school, appear also to have followed its practice of handling the Italian Neo-Platonists' theories of beauty and love (e.g., the different stages of beauty) in the sonnet form. A close translation of the language of French sonnets by Spenser would ordinarily have been some evidence of the likelihood of his imitation of their treatment of Platonic ideas. But Spenser has not literally translated the language of those French sonnets which might have furnished him with models of the treatment of Platonic ideas in the

---

[1] See *ante* Chapter V.

*Amoretti;* he has been more faithful in rendering other sonnets of the French masters.[1] Yet the resemblance, in respect of shades of ideas and the mode of their treatment, between some of Spenser's sonnets and those of the French school, does suggest some connection between the two. Some of Spenser's sonnets have indeed similarity of phrasing with Tasso's and Tebaldeo's and a few of the Platonising sonnets[2] of the *Amoretti* have on this ground been traced to these Italian poets as their source. Tebaldeo (1463-1537) was a close follower of Petrarch and described, after his master, the lady of his sonnets as a sublime ideal. Tasso too followed this common practice but associated gentleness and moral purity with ideal beauty. None of these poets can be regarded as a Platonist in any special sense and possibly none was influenced by the Renaissance theories of beauty and love developed by Ficinus, Castiglione and Pico. There is no justification, therefore, for tracing the Platonism of Spenser's *Amoretti* to Tebaldeo and

---

[1] For example, Sir Sidney Lee points out the similarity in language between sonnet no. XV of the *Amoretti* and sonnet no. XXXII of Desportes' *Diane*, I and between sonnets no. LXXV and LXIX of the *Amoretti* and Ronsard's *Sonnets pour Hélène*, II.

[2] Sonnets no. 3, 22, 45. See *Modern Language Review*, Vol. XXII. p. 194.

Tasso, though his indebtedness to them or to others like Serafino and some Latin poets in respect of his language and forms of expression, may not be quite improbable.

Grades of beauty as postulated in Pico and Castiglione and adopted by Spenser in his Hymns, appear also in the *Amoretti* under the influence of the French sonneteers. The lines of demarcation separating the different grades are not indeed very clear either in the French sonnets or in the *Amoretti* and the grades do not always strictly correspond to those in Pico or Castiglione. There may be room for difference of opinion as to the extent of the obligation of the French sonneteers to the Italian Neo-Platonists and the question may also arise as to how far Spenser's *Amoretti* followed directly, like his Hymns, the gradation of beauty in the Italian Neo-Platonists and how far they imitated the treatment of it in the French sonnets of the Pléiade. Yet the resemblance between the *Amoretti* and some of these French sonnets in respect of their handling of the Neo-Platonic stages of beauty, deserves notice. The first grade, i.e., the full impression of the beauty of the beloved on the lover's mind is hinted at by Pontus de Thyard in a sonnet in his *Les Erreurs Amoureuses* where he contrasts the impression of the lady's face on the lover's heart with her portrait. The contrast is thus expressed:

> Quelqu'un voyant la belle pourtraiture
> De ton visage en un tableau depeinte,
> S'emerveilloit de chose si bien feinte,
> Et qui suivoit de si près la nature.
>
> Helás, pensay-je, Amour par sa pointure,
> A mieux en moy cette beauté emprainte
> Cette beauté tant cruellement sainte,
> Que, l'adorant, elle me devient dure.
>
> Car ce tableau par main d'homme tracé,
> Au fil des ans pourroit estre effacé,
> Ou obscurci, perdant sa couleur vive :
>
> Mais la memoire, emprainte en ma pensée,
> De sa beauté ne peut estre effacée
> Au laps du temps, au moins tant que je vive.'

Spenser refers to this impression in the first quatrain of sonnet no. 45 of the *Amoretti* :

> 'Leave, lady! in your glasse of cristall clene,
> Your goodly *selfe*, for evermore to vew :
> And in my selfe my inward selfe, I meane,
> Most lively lyke behold your semblant trew.'[1]

The impression on the lover's 'inward selfe' is here described as identical with the reflection on the mirror for which it is to be the substitute. In the next few lines of this sonnet, the poet goes

[1] These four lines have also been traced to Tebaldeo. See *Modern Language Review*, Vol. XXII. p. 194.

beyond the preliminary stage and conceives of the beloved's beauty as something more than a photographic reproduction of her physical features.

This higher grade of beauty is reached when the lover's mind invests the beloved with ideal charms and offers its homage to her as to a superior being. The lover has now before him an image of beauty which is more lovely than the reflection of the lady on the mirror. Sonnet no. 45 mentions later the superior beauty of this image :

> '—were it not that, through your cruelty,
>   With sorrow dimmed and deform'd *it* were, (i.e. the heart)
>   The goodly *ymage* of your visnomy,
>   *Clearer* then cristall, would therein appere.'

Elsewhere the worship of the image of ideal beauty is thus hinted at :

> ' Her temple fayre is built within my *mind*,
>   In which her *glorious ymage* placed is ;
>   On which my thoughts doo day and night attend,
>   Lyke sacred priests that never thinke amisse ! '

One of Desportes'[1] sonnets has been pointed out as the model of sonnet no. 22 of the *Amoretti* from

---

[1] No. 43 of *Diane*, I.

which the above lines are taken.[1] Desportes' sonnet is quoted below :

> ' Solitaire et pensif, dans un bois ecarté,
> Bien loin du populaire et de la tourbe espesse,
> Je veux bastir un temple à ma fiere déesse,
> Pour apprendre mes vœux à sa divinité.
> Là, de jour et de nuit, par moy sera chanté
> Le pouvoir de ses yeux, sa gloire et sa hautesse ;
> Et devot, son beau nom j'invoqueray sans cesse,
> Quand je seray pressé de quelque adversité.
> Mon œil sera la lampe ardant continuelle,
> Devant *l'image saint d'une dame si belle ;*
> Mon corps sera l'autel, et mes soupirs les vœux.
> Par mille et mille vers je chanteray l'office,
> Puis, espanchant mes pleurs et coupant mes cheveux,
> J'y feray tous les jours de mon cœur sacrifice.

A devotional note has been struck in both the poems and the reference to the temple, sacrifice etc., is quite in keeping with it. But the idea that underlies this note should not pass unnoticed. There is a clear mention in each sonnet of the image[2] of beauty—'glorious ymage' or 'l'image

---

[1] See *Modern Language Review*, Vol. IV. p. 67. But Tasso has also been referred to as a possible source.

[2] About the image Castiglione says,

'... 'l Cortegiano con l'aiuto della ragione ... e dentro nella imaginazione la (bellezza) formi astratta da ogni materia ; e cosí la faccia amica e cara all'anima sua, ed ivi la goda, . . . . ' (*Il Cortegiano*, Libro Quarto, LXVI).

saint d' une dame si belle'—which the lover sets up in his inner being.

The other grades of the Neo-Platonists are beauty of the mind of the beloved, beauty not of any particular woman but of womanhood in general, beauty realised as an inherent part of the lover's soul and universal intellectual beauty. All these are mentioned by them as symbolising distinct stages of the soul's upward march and the French school has also drawn upon these striking conceptions in its sonnets. Du Bellay, for example, expressly mentions the beauty of the spirit or of the mind in sonnet no. 2 of the *Sonnets de l' Honneste Amour* :

> ' Ce ne sont pas ces beaux cheveux dorez,
> Ni ce beau front, qui l'honneur mesme honore :
> Ce ne sont pas les deux archers encore
> De ses beaux yeux de cent yeux adorez;
> Ce ne sont pas les deux brins colorez
> De ce coral, ces levres que j'adore ;
> Ce n'est ce teint emprunté de l'aurore
> Ni autre objet des cœurs enamourez ;
> Ce ne sont pas ni ces lis ni ces roses,
> Ni ces deux rangs de perles bien closes ;
> C'est cest *esprit*, rare present des cieux,
> Dont la beaulté de cent graces pourveue
> Perce mon ame et mon cœur et mes yeux
> Par les rayons de sa poignante veue.'

# THE *AMORETTI*

In sonnet no. 79 of the *Amoretti* Spenser defines true beauty as '*the gentle wit,* And vertuous *mind*' :

> ' Men call you fayre, and you doe credit it,
> For that your selfe ye dayly such doe see :
> *But the trew fayre, that is the gentle wit,*
> *And vertuous mind,* is much more praysd of me :
> For all the rest, how ever fayre it be,
> Shall turne to nought and loose that glorious hew :
> But onely that is permanent and free
> From frayle corruption, that doth flesh ensew.
> That is true beautie :'

Spenser next realises a still higher grade of beauty which is not an external object of vision, but is part of his own soul. He says :

> ' I seeke her bowre with her late presence deckt;
> Yet nor in field nor bowre I her can fynd ;
> Yet field and bowre are full of her aspect :
> But, when myne eyes I thereunto direct,
> They ydly back returne to me agayne :
> And, when I hope to see theyr trew object,
> I fynd my selfe but fed with fancies vayne.
> *Ceasse then, myne eyes,* to seeke her selfe to see ;
> And let *my thoughts* behold her selfe *in mee.*'

The eyes are here forbidden to seek for the beloved and the thoughts of the lover apprehend her beauty as part of his mind.

Desportes arrives at the identical conception of beauty as part of the lover's mind in the following lines :

> ' Pourquoy si folement croyez-vous à un verre,
>   Voulant voir les beautez que vous avez des cieux ?
>   Mirez-vous dessus moy pour les connoistre mieux,
>   Et voyez de quels traits vostre bel œil m'enferre.'

A more sublime grade is reached when intelligible beauty of the most universal type is realised as an absolute entity through the power of contemplation. It is this beauty that is the prime source of all earthly beauty. The Pléiade sonneteers mean this abstract entity by the term 'L'Idée'. Pontus de Thyard calls it sapience and mentions it as the Universal Idea :

> ' Père divin, sapience eternelle,
> Commencement et fin de toute chose,
> Où en pourtrait indeleble repose
> De l'Univers, *l'Idée* universelle.'

Du Bellay is less abstruse when he refers to 'L'Idée' as the source of that beauty which people adore in this world :

> ' Que songes-tu, mon ame emprisonnée ?
> Pourquoi te plais l'obscur de nostre jour
> Si pour voler en un plus clair sejour
> Tu as au dos l'aile bien empennée ?

Là est le bien que tout esprit desire,
Là le repos où tout le monde aspire,
Là est l'amour, là le plaisir encore.
Là, ô mon ame, au plus haut ciel guidée
Tu y pourras recognoistre *l'Idée*
De la beauté, qu'en ce monde j'adore.'

Desportes too sings of the Idea as the origin of the beloved's beauty :—

'Sur la plus belle Idée au ciel vous fustes faite,
Voulant nature un jour monstrer tout son pouvoir,
Depuis vous luy servez de forme et de miroir,
Et toute autre beauté sur la vostre est portraite.'[1]

Pontus de Thyard describes the 'Idée' as being approachable by the spirit alone and as the model of the beauty of his beloved. He says :

'Mon esprit ha heureusement porté
Au plus beau ciel sa force outrecuidée
Pour s'abbreuver en la plus belle *Idée*
D'où le pourtrait j'ai pris de ta beauté,' etc.[2]

Spenser regards the Idea of Beauty as realisable only through contemplation and as filling the lover's mind without any appeal to his eyes.

'Since I have lackt the comfort of that light,
The which was wont to lead my thoughts astray ;
I wander as in darkenesse of the night,
Affrayd of every dangers least dismay.

[1] Sonnet no. 67 of *Diane*, II.
[2] Sonnet no. 33 of *Les Erreurs Amoureuses*, Bk. III.

## 192  PLATONIC IDEAS IN SPENSER

> Ne ought I see, though in the clearest day,
> When others gaze upon theyr shadowes vayne,
> But th' onely image of that heavenly ray,
> Whereof some glance doth in mine eie remayne.
> Of which beholding the Idæa playne,
> Through contemplation of my purest part,
> With light thereof I doe my selfe sustayne,
> And thereon feed my love-affamisht hart.
> But, with such brightnesse whylest I *fill my mind*,
> I *starve my body*, and mine *eyes doe blynd*.'[1]

The French expression 'L'Idée' by which is meant the Platonic Idea, is responsible for the anagrams *Délie* (the title of the work of Scève published in 1544) and *Delia* (Daniel's sonnet-cycle published in 1594). The title of Drayton's sonnet-cycle 'Idea'[2] published in 1603, was suggested by *'L'Idée'* of Claude de Pontoux (1579).[3]

The gradual elevation of the human soul above the earthly plane and its final absorption in Divinity is a well-known creed of Neo-Platonism. According to the Italian amorists of the Renaissance like Castiglione and Bembo, it is beauty's touch that removes the impurity of the soul and

---

[1] Sonnet no. 87 of the *Amoretti*.
[2] The full title of another series is ' *Idea's Mirror*.'
[3] For the use of the Platonic Idea in Elizabethan literature, reference may be made to Elton's *Michael Drayton, a critical study*, p. 47.

raises it up to higher and still higher stages till the Supreme Beauty is reached.  Desire for this consummation finds expression in Ronsard, Du Bellay and Pontus de Thyard.[1]  Ronsard calls beauty the fire that removes the dross of the flesh and brings out the pure gold of the spirit.  He says :

> ' Je veux brusler, pour m'en-voler aux Cieux,
> Tout l'imparfait de ceste escorce humaine,
> M'éternisant comme le fils d'Alcmeine,
> Qui tout en feu s'assit entre les Dieux.
> Ja mon esprit, chatouillé de son mieux,
> Dedans ma chair rebelle se promeine,
> Et ja le bois de sa victime ameine
> Pour s'enflammer aux rayons de tes yeux.
> O saint brasier ! ô feu chastement beau !
> Las ! brule moi d'un si chaste flambeau,
> Qu' abandonnant ma depouille connue,
> Net, libre et nud, je vole d'un plein saut
> Jusques au Ciel, pour adorer là haut
> *L'autre beauté* dont la tienne est venue !'[2]

Du Bellay sings :

> ' Ces deux soleilz, deux flambeaux de mon âme,
> Pour me rejoindre à la divinité,
> Percent l'obscur de mon humanité
> Par les rayons de leur jumelle flâme.'[3]

---

[1] *Cf.* sonnet no. 33 of Bk. III. of *Les Erreurs Amoureuses.*
[2] Sonnet no. 167 of Bk. I. of the *Amours.*
[3] Sonnet no. 5 of *Œuvres*, Vol. II. p. 62. *Cf.* sonnet no. 6 of *Œuvres*, Vol. II.

Though, unlike his last two Hymns, Spenser's *Amoretti* are free from mysticism, they recognise the power of beauty for purifying the human soul and uplifting it to a sublime region. Sonnet no. 3 of the cycle has these lines :

> ' The soverayne beauty which I doo admyre,
> Witnesse the world how worthy to be prayzed !
> The light whereof hath kindled heavenly fyre
> In my fraile spirit, by her from *basenesse raysed* ;
> That, being now with her huge brightnesse dazed,
> Base thing I can no more endure to view : '

Sonnet no. 80 refers to the elevation of the soul to the spiritual plane. The poet sings :

> ' —give leave to me, in pleasant mew
> To sport my muse, and sing my loves sweet praise ;
> The *contemplation* of whose heavenly hew,
> My spirit to an *higher pitch will rayse*—'[1]

In one of the sonnets (no. 79) Spenser adverts to the opposite idea and mentions the derivation[2] of the human soul from the ultimate source of beauty,

> ' —that fayre Spirit, from whom al true
> And *perfect beauty did at first proceed* :
> He onely fayre, and what he fayre hath made—'

---

[1] This poem has also been traced to Virgil. See *Modern Language Review*, Vol. XXII. p. 195.

[2] This may be based on the philosophical theory of emanation. See *ante* Chapter VI.

## THE *AMORETTI*

There are no doubt frequent references to the descent of the soul from its heavenly home in Ficinus and Pico ; but one of the sonneteers of the Pléiade also, viz., Pontus de Thyard, thus speaks of his lady's spirit as coming down from the fairest heavens :

'Du plus beau Ciel, ton esprit descendu,' etc.

Though Platonic ideas in the *Amoretti* have in many cases come through the medium of French sonnets of the sixteenth century, there are instances of direct borrowing from Plato in this sonnet-cycle. For example, the vision of beauty causing amazement and dazing the senses of the lover in sonnet no. 3, appears to have been suggested by the *Phaedrus,* though Tasso is also referred to as a possible source of this particular sonnet.

# BIBLIOGRAPHY

**Ariosto, L.** *Orlando Furioso,* translated into English by W. S. Rose. 2 Vols. London, 1892-95.

**Aristotle.** *The Nicomachean Ethics of Aristotle,* translated into English by J. E. C. Welldon. London, 1912.

**Aristotle.** *The Ethics of Aristotle,* translated into English by D. P. Chase. Oxford, 1847. Revised by T. W. R. and published in the Scott Library Series.

**Bembo, Pietro.** *Degli Asolani.* Milano.

**Benivieni, Girolamo.** *Ode of Love,* translated into English by J. B. Fletcher in *Modern Philology,* Vol. VIII. 1911.

**Bruno, Giordano.** *The Heroic Enthusiasts,* translated into English by L. Williams. 2 Vols. London, 1887.

**Calvin, John.** *Institutes,* translated into English.

*Cambridge History of English Literature,* Vol. III. Cambridge, 1913.

**Carpenter, F. I.** *A Reference Guide to Edmund Spenser.* Chicago, 1923.

**Castiglione, Baldesar.** *Il Cortegiano.* 1893.

**Cavalcanti.** 'Ode of Love,' translated into English in *Modern Philology,* Vol. VII. 1910.

**Church, R. W.** *Spenser* in the E.M.L. Series. London, 1909.

**Claude de Pontoux.** *L'Idée.*

**Courthope, W. J.** *History of English Poetry,* Vol. II. London, 1926.

**De Moss, W. F.** 'Spenser's Twelve Moral Virtues "According to Aristotle" ', in *Modern Philology,* Vol. XVI. 1918.

**Desportes, P.** *Diane,* I and *Diane,* II.

## BIBLIOGRAPHY

De Vere, Aubrey Thomas. 'Characteristics of Spenser's Poetry' and 'Spenser as a Philosophic Poet', in *Essays, chiefly on Poetry*. 2 Vols. London, 1887.
*Dictionary of Religion and Ethics*. Article on Holiness.
Dowden, Edward. *Transcripts and Studies*. London, 1910.
Du Bellay, Joachim. *Sonnets de l'Honneste Amour*.
Du Bellay, Joachim. *Œuvres*.
Einstein, Lewis. *The Italian Renaissance in England*. New York, 1913.
Elton, Oliver. *Modern Studies*. London, 1907.
Ficinus, Marsilio. 'Commentarium in Convivium', in *Omnia Divini Platonis Opera*. Basileae, 1551.
Ficinus, Marsilio. *Plotini Divini illius Platonica familia Philosophi De rebus Philosophicis*. Basileae, MDLIX.
Fletcher, J. B. 'Mr. Sidney Lee and Spenser's Amoretti', in *Modern Language Notes*, Vol. XVIII. 1903.
Fletcher, J. B. 'Dante's Second Love', in *Modern Philology*, Vol. XIII. 1915.
Greenlaw, E. 'Review', in *Modern Language Notes*, Vol. XLV. p. 327. 1930.
Hales, J. W. 'Edmund Spenser', in the Globe Edition of the *Works of Edmund Spenser*. London, 1910.
Harrison, J. S. *Platonism in English Poetry*. New York and London, 1903.
Holme, J. W. 'Italian Courtesy-Books of the Sixteenth Century', in *Modern Language Review*, Vol. V. 1910.
Inge, W. R. *Christian Mysticism*. London, 1912. The Bampton Lectures, 1899.
Inge, W. R. *Philosophy of Plotinus*. 2 Vols. London, 1923.
Jones, H. S. V. 'The Faerie Queene and the Mediaeval Aristotelian tradition', in *Journal of English and Germanic Philology*, Vol. XXV. 1926.

## 198  PLATONIC IDEAS IN SPENSER

Jusserand, J. J. 'Spenser's Twelve Private Morall Virtues as Aristotle hath devised', in *Modern Philology*, Vol. III. 1906.

Kastner, L. E. 'Spenser's "Amoretti" and Desportes', in *Modern Language Review*, Vol. IV. 1908.

Lee, Sir Sidney. *Elizabethan Sonnets*. 2 Vols. Westminster, 1904.

Lee, Sir Sidney. *The French Renaissance in England*. New York, 1910.

Legouis, E. *Spenser*. London and Toronto, 1926.

Long, P. W. 'Spenser and Lady Carey', in *Modern Language Review*, Vol. III. 1908.

Lowell, J. R. 'Spenser' in *Works*, Vol. IV.

Kerr, W. A. R. 'The Pléiade and Platonism', in *Modern Philology*, Vol. V. 1908.

Mirandola, Pico della. *A Platonick Discourse upon Love*, translated into English by T. Stanley and published in the Humanist's Library. London, 1912.

More, E. P. *Hellenistic Philosophies*. London, 1923.

Nenna, G. B. *Il Nennio*. MDXLII.

Osgood, C. G. *A Concordance to the Poems of Edmund Spenser*. Washington, 1915.

Owen, John. *Sceptics of the Italian Renaissance*. London and New York, 1893.

Padelford, F. M. 'The Women in Spenser's Allegory of Love', in *Journal of English and Germanic Philology*, Vol. XVI. 1917.

Padelford, F. M. 'Spenser and the Theology of Calvin', in *Modern Philology*, Vol. XII. 1914.

Padelford, F. M. 'The Spiritual Allegory of the Faerie Queene, Book One', in *Journal of English and Germanic Philology*, Vol. XXII. 1923.

Padelford, F. M. 'Spenser's Fowre Hymnes', in *Journal*

## BIBLIOGRAPHY 199

of *English and Germanic Philology*, Vol. XIII. 1914.

Petrarch, F. *Some Love Songs of Petrarch*, translated into English by W. D. Foulke. Oxford, 1892.

Plato. *Dialogues of Plato*, translated by B. Jowett. 5 Vols. Oxford, 1892.

Plotinus. *An Essay on the Beautiful*, translated by T. Taylor. London, 1917.

Plotinus. *Select Works of Plotinus*, translated into English by T. Taylor. London, 1929.

Pontus de Thyard. *Les Erreurs Amoureuses*.

Renwick, W. L. 'The Critical Origins of Spenser's Diction', in *Modern Language Review*, Vol. XVII. 1922.

Renwick, W. L. *Edmund Spenser, an Essay on Renaissance Poetry*. London, 1925.

Romei, A. *Discorsi*. Ferrara, MDLXXXVI.

Ronsard, P. *Sonnets pour Hélène*, II.

Ronsard, P. *Amours*, I.

Sawtelle, Alice E. *The Sources of Spenser's Classical Mythology*. New York, 1896.

Scott, J. G. 'The Sources of Spenser's Amoretti', in *Modern Language Review*, Vol. XXII. 1927.

Scott, Mary Augusta. *Elizabethan Translations from the Italian*. Boston and New York, 1916.

Smith, J. C. 'The Problem of Spenser's Sonnets', in *Modern Language Review*, Vol. V. 1910.

Shelley, P. B. 'Hymn to Intellectual Beauty'.

Spenser, Edmund. 'Complete Works in Prose and Verse', edited by A. B. Grosart. 10 Vols. Blackburn, 1882-84.

Spenser, Edmund. *Works of Edmund Spenser*. The Globe Edition. London, 1910.

Spenser, Edmund. *Faerie Queene,* Book I. edited by G. W. Kitchin. London, 1886.
Spenser, Edmund. *Faerie Queene,* Bk. II. edited by G. W. Kitchen. London, 1899.
Spenser, Edmund. *Faerie Queene,* Bk. I. edited by H. M. Percival. London and New York, 1893.
Spenser, Edmund. *Faerie Queene,* Bk. I. edited by L. Winstanley. Cambridge, 1915.
Spenser, Edmund. *Faerie Queene,* Bk. II. edited by L. Winstanley. Cambridge, 1914.
Spenser, Edmund. *Fowre Hymnes,* edited by L. Winstanley. Cambridge, 1907.
Spenser, Edmund. *Shepheardes Calender,* edited by C. H. Herford. London and New York, 1895.
Spenser, Edmund. *Faerie Queene,* Bk. V. edited by Kate M. Warren. Westminster, 1904.
Stewart, J. A. 'Platonism in English Poetry', in *English Literature and the Classics.* Oxford, 1912.
Symonds, J. A. 'Dantesque and Platonic Love', in *Contemporary Review,* Vol. LVIII. 1890.
Symonds, J. A. *Renaissance in Italy.* 7 Vols. London, 1926.
Tasso, T. *Jerusalem Delivered,* translated into English by E. Fairfax. 2 Vols. London, 1844.
Taylor, A. E. 'Spenser's Knowledge of Plato', in *Modern Language Review,* Vol. XIX. 1924.
Tilley, M. P. 'The Comedy of Lingua and the Faerie Queene', in *Modern Language Notes,* Vol. XLII. 1927.
Winbolt, S. E. *Spenser and his Poetry.* London, 1912.

38610 ST. MARY'S COLLEGE OF MARYLAND
ST. MARY'S CITY, MARYLAND